44 Soccer Striker Mistakes to Avoid

Mirsad Hasic

DEDICATION

I dedicate this book to my wife.

CONTENTS

ACKNOWLEDGMENTS

I would like to thank my family for their support.

Introduction

For those who may not be familiar with my work, allow me to explain a bit about my approach and style.

Firstly, I bring as much real-world information to the pages as I possibly can.

I like to get personally involved because you're going to be involved, so I need to know what it is that you'll be going through.

What this means is that there's very little in my books that I have not researched thoroughly and experienced personally.

I then pass on my findings and experiences, whenever appropriate, which is something that helps me to connect better with you, my audience.

Why this Book?

After looking through other books aimed at covering the common mistakes made by soccer strikers, it was clear to me that there was definitely more than enough room for another book on the topic.

Just about every book that I looked through was typical of most of the so-called "soccer guides" in that they were too impersonal, overly complicated, and only focused on how to do a thing.

There was very little cover on how to avoid making common mistakes, the very things that often hinder or prevent a striker from progressing and developing his game still further.

This guide avoids regurgitating the same old stuff under a new title. My book, now your book too, contains real life examples of the actual things that most strikers and wannabe strikers fail to recognize as they attempt to sharpen their game.

This book is all about the details, exposing those overlooked mistakes that often halt or hinder the progress of anyone trying to improve as a soccer striker, be that at the amateur or professional level.

Your success depends on whether or not you get to catch these all too common setbacks in your purist to become the best striker that you can possibly be.

Follow the guidance on these pages and you will leave no stone unturned. Take note and adhere to the principles as they are presented in these chapters and you will get to develop your striker skills and take your game up to a whole new level.

Why Other Books Fail to Deliver

One of the main reasons why so many of the other soccer striker guides fail to deliver is because they are too broad in their approach and to assuming of their readership.

These books are typically full of drills which all promise to reveal the true art of scoring more goals. Even when their instructions are correct, they tend to be overly complicated.

Furthermore, I find that a lot of these books contain far too much unnecessary information, basic stuff that any beginner coach can teach you to do during a regular training session.

My impression is that the authors stuff anything halfway-related into their books as a way to pad them out.

In short, most of the striker guides out there are boring and make simple instructions way too technical; hence the need for something new.

This book is complementary to what you can do in training. It contains details that only the luckiest of strikers get to find out about. These chapters will open your eyes to what's right and what's wrong in the world of successful goal scoring.

The succeeding pages will make you aware of many mistakes and typical blunders, most of which you won't have been introduced to. These are potential areas for failure and setbacks that you would never have picked up on if it weren't for this book.

Welcome to "44 Striker Mistakes to Avoid."

I, We, and You…

You will notice throughout this book how I write in the first person, "I," quite a lot. This is deliberate; it is to make your journey more interesting and the reading experience less pressuring.

There are too many coldly-written soccer books on sale today, and that's one approach I make sure to avoid. The "I" accounts in this book are more likely to get your focus too, as you will undoubtedly relate to some of the things that I write about on a personal level.

I also use "we" on occasions as well. This is because I have been where you are at now, to a greater or lesser extent, and know what you're going through. Therefore we're in this together, and that helps you to pick up on similarities much easier.

I also use the "you" approach because I'm addressing you, my reader, directly.

How to Approach This Book?

This book is designed to make you aware of the tiny errors, the little slips that can make a big difference in whether you succeed as a striker or not. These are the very things that can, when gone unnoticed, have a huge negative impact on the way you perform as a player.

This book will also make you aware of the problems associated with your belief system. These are the little messages which govern your thoughts, words, and your actions, or inactions, as the case may be.

Strikers who perform below par often fall short not because they lack the physical talent, but more often because they don't truly believe in themselves.

The primary purpose of my book is to open your mind to the things that you haven't been aware of before.

Here you will discover new ideas, the best practices, and get to develop a sharper overall awareness for the striker position. You are going to learn what to look out for as you develop your game.

Equally as important is that you will also discover what to watch out for. This ensures that you don't fall prey to the often latent traps that can hinder or even reverse any attempts you make to become the great striker that you dream of being.

OK, so without further ado let's get started. Positive change is coming your way and it begins right now.

1. Not Taking the "Assistant" Role

A very important ability to have in modern soccer nowadays is what I call "the assisting striker" skill. Because tactics can change so quickly on the field, the modern player has to be able to seamlessly fit into different roles at various times during a game.

It's important therefore, that you can adjust your style of play at the drop of a hat so that it benefits both you and your team as a whole.

This "assisting striker" approach is not like the false no.9 of Leo Messi. What I'm talking about here is a bit different. This is because Messi's skills and physical composition require him to stay out of, and not inside, the penalty area. Messi is a smart dribbler and one of the most, if not the most, skillful soccer players to ever touch a ball.

However, Messi is a dribbler and depends on his speed and footwork to conquer the opposite team's defense. He is not the pure 1.85m striker who relies on his striking power and headers to meet his objectives.

Messi is certainly not Zlatan Ibrahimović (Swedish professional striker for French club Paris Saint-Germain and the Swedish national team) or Miroslav Klose (German striker for Serie A club Lazio) or Robert Lewandowski (Polish professional striker for Bayern Munich and captain of the Poland national team). Messi is none of these, he's someone totally different.

If you are more of the Ibrahimović type and less of the Messi type, then you need to be prepared to play different roles in the game, especially if your team's tactics and playing style is based chiefly on attacking and excessive passing.

Some will argue that a pure striker must stick to the penalty area as much as possible since this is the best place for him to shine. This seems like a perfectly reasonable and logical argument too. However, nothing is ever that clear cut as I will now explain.

In Ibrahimović's book "I Am Zlatan" the Swedish extraordinary striker speaks in one chapter about what he called his "aha" moment, or the moment of shining.

It was when the Italian coach Fabio Capello (the coach of Juventus at that time), took him on a solo training session and ordered him to stick to the penalty area and never leave it no matter what.

From there, the coach had the ball boys send him passes and crosses from all angles. Ibrahimović said that his performance began to improve dramatically after this, so much so that he began to double and sometimes triple the number of goals he scored compared to when he used to leave the penalty area.

When Capello explained his decision for keeping Ibrahimović inside the penalty area, he said that a striker like Ibrahimović, who possesses such shooting power and great finishing skills, is better staying in the penalty box no matter what else is going on around him. Guess what?

He was right too, or at least the right decision for the team he was playing for at the time. It was the beginning of Ibrahimović's era; 10 years of pure domination and success, from 2005 through till the present day, at the time of writing this book.

However, all this happened when he was playing for Juventus not for Barcelona, which brings me to my point.

You see, when Ibrahimović moved to Barcelona in 2009, Pep Guardiola (Barcelona's coach at that time) had a certain playing style known as Tiki–Taka (also spelled tiqui-taca). Tiki–Taka is a style of play in soccer, characterized by short passing and quick movements, working the ball through various channels while maintaining possession.

So the ball got passed around a lot as the game centered around the forward Messi. That meant Pep Guardiola had to use Ibrahimović's points of strength so that he became a part of the broader team effort, albeit at the expense of his goal scoring record and ability from within the penalty box.

Ibrahimović's now had to change roles, and leverage his receiving as well as his passing and assisting skills. It took him some time but he got there in the end, and he became a true asset to the team with his newly developed style of play.

However, Ibrahimović left Barcelona the following year, in 2010, after just one season. The player's sudden departure from the club was something of a controversial decision at the time.

Some say he quit because he didn't want to overshadow Lionel Messi, others say he had problems with coach Guardiola (more likely), claiming that his former boss used to bully him.

Anyway, Ibrahimović went to join Inter Milan where he was the team's main striker. The recent shift in his playing style (the things he had learned in his short time at Barcelona), had really helped him to raise his game.

He had, in fact, become a truly "complete" player as a consequence of his one season at that club, so the experience was not all bad. In other words, he was very good before but he had now become a true soccer sensation.

If you have followed Ibrahimović's history and performance with different teams since the start of his professional career, like I have (I've been following his career since he was playing in Ajax Amsterdam, back in his early days), then you will really notice the different in the way he plays now compared to the way he used to play. The difference really is quite dramatic.

When Ibrahimović began his career he was undoubtedly a good striker, though not all that good at assisting generally, yet he still insisted in playing outside the box.

Then his coach, Fabio Capello, sharpened his game and his goal scoring skills by forcing him to stick to the penalty area and not stray from it. Later, when he went to play at Barcelona, Ibrahimović had to change his style yet again, this time assisting other teammates. All these things combined over time are what helped him to eventually develop into a complete player.

Let's take another example, this time the French striker Olivier Giroud.

Now I probably watch too many Arsenal games, but then I would do because I'm a big fan. Giroud, for me, is nothing more than a slightly above average attacking player who is lucky enough to play professional soccer.

Nevertheless, how did a slightly above average striker get to play for the premier League soccer club Arsenal F.C.? Well, the reason is quite obvious if you know what to look for. Giroud has a very valuable skill, and that is his ability to play and act as an attacking station outside the penalty area.

Despite scoring an average number of goals per year (15-20 in more than 45 games) he's still a valued Arsenal player, in spite of his lack of speed. He has nothing to offer by way of extraordinary finishing skills either.

Furthermore, Giroud suffers from an extreme drop in performance toward the end of every season. Yet despite all of these setbacks he is still a valuable asset. This would be the same for any striker who knows how to assist and help his teammates score more goals.

If you watch his games with both Arsenal and France, you will see Giroud frequently creating breakaways for his teammates, sending lethal through passes with both his head and his feet.

Giroud created one of the most wonderful goals you could ever hope to witness in an Arsenal game. Here, he assisted his teammate, central midfielder Jack Wilshere, by executing a spectacular above the ground back–heel pass in the middle of five rival players.

You might want to take a look for yourself, so just search online for the term "Wilshere's goal vs. Norwich City".

Now onto my point to explain why I'm bothering to mention all of this. It is because I need to highlight the importance of becoming complete, and that means sharpening your assisting skills.

This includes improving your passes, developing a better overall awareness of your teammate's positions on the field, and the ability to be able to communicate with them without talking.

In other words, you need to know how to read the game in advance, and then rapidly connect the dots to create opportunities for your team players to score.

2. Failure to Practice Header Skills

In order to be exceptional you must be great at something, have some sort of an extraordinary skill that sets you apart from the rest. If you fail to improve you header skill, then you are failing to progress your game in a very important area.

I believe that quality headers and air plays are reasonably easy to master and are something that anyone can become renowned for if only they practice enough in this area. Not so many do though, which means there is plenty of room you to excel and stand out in this important area of the game.

Having an edge, and being widely recognized for your great ability to deal with crosses, set pieces, and high through balls, will easily make you an important asset to any team.

Quite often a team will favor a competent air play master and someone who's really good at headers over other, more skilled attackers. This is especially the case when the attacking strategy of a team is to exploit long balls and headers as part of their tactical play.

OK, let us look at a real-world example of this to illustrate the point:

In 2005, the English team, Tottenham Hotspur F.C (Spurs) bought an Egyptian player called Mido. Now, this Egyptian striker had been having some ups and downs at the time, scoring zero goals during his last season in Italy.

He had, for all intents and purposes, lost his way and somehow needed rediscovering. Well, Tottenham's then manager Martin Jol decided to do just that with a creative idea he had.

Mido (1.9m) had played in Ajax Amsterdam's academy, right next to striker Ibrahimović. He had also partnered with Ivorian striker Didier Drogba for two successful years in Marseille.

Mido was renowned as being one of the best players in Europe when it came to headers and air plays. These were skills that Tottenham's main strikers Robbie Keane and Jermain Defoe both lacked.

Both Keane and Defoe were quick, but they were quite short too (Keane at 1.75m and Defoe at 1.67m).

Spur's Dutch manager decided that these two weren't enough and that he needed someone like Mido to add to the depth of his quad.

He didn't want to sell any of his star players to make room for Mido, but rather blend all three of them in on his new game plan, so here's what he did.

He made Mido into a target player where he instructed all other players to cross long balls to him. He would then assist the fast striker who was playing with him at the top end, where he would either:

a) Put him in a one-to-one situation against opponents where he could easily dribble or run past them.

b) Create a situation where he could run in from behind and use his speed to out run the opponent's defenders.

Alternatively, Mido could also use his strong physique to hold onto the ball and wait for the rest of the team to move up before making his play.

On his first two seasons at Tottenham Hotspur, Mido managed to score 17 goals and participated in 30 out of 90 other goals scored by his two attacking teammates.

Mastering Explosive Jumps

If you're a keen soccer fan, and I'm sure you are if you're reading this book, then you will have definitely seen Cristiano Ronaldo jumping or performing spectacular headers during his games.

You can learn a lot from watching his videos and by studying his jumping and heading styles.

Ronaldo is the "complete Portuguese" (that's what his fans like to call him), and is currently one of the best jumpers and headers in the whole of Europe, even though he's not that tall at just 1.85m. Even so, his take-off and jumping style is the envy of his peers.

Not only he can jump higher than any giant defender marking him, Ronaldo also has the ability to strike his headers with the just right power and in the right direction without needing too much space to prepare for his jump. That's truly remarkable when you think about it.

This Real Madrid star is impressive at mastering high balls, but you know what is even more impressive? He wasn't playing like this just a few years ago. I can remember seeing Ronaldo at Manchester United in the Premier league, and although he was good, he wasn't that good.

Ronaldo was still developing as a player while he was at Manchester United (118 goals in 292 games), and he only really came into his own at Real Madrid (313 goals in 300 games).

The impressive jumps and headers that you see Ronaldo making every week with Real Madrid did not just happen naturally.

This is not some kind of latent talent that just came to surface one day. He had to work at it, and he worked extremely hard to become the best that he could possibly be.

What you see now is the result of someone who worked relentlessly on further developing his skills. Ronaldo was so eager to enhance his performance that he asked a guy like Usain Bolt (the fastest man on earth) to teach him how to improve his speed.

Furthermore, he used to get lessons from professional NBA players to teach him how to jump better, thus making full use of his body to make explosive take–offs.

Patience, relentless commitment, and a sheer determination to succeed are the things that have made Ronaldo the great player that he is right now.

No wonder he has three Ballon D'ors (an annual association soccer award given by FIFA to the male player considered to have performed the best in the previous calendar year) and a 19 million dollar annual salary.

It just goes to show what can be accomplished by having the right attitude and approach to succeed.

The Jump

If you get to master explosive jumps or power jumps, then great things will come to pass for you and your game. In fact, I have seen players from both sides (defenders and attackers) scoring spectacular headers despite being shorter than the opposition defenders who are marking them.

Let's take a look at how you begin to work at improving in this area.

Boosting your jumping power really needs to start in a gym. This is because you need to exercise the muscles responsible for the jumping mechanism of your body, namely the abs, the legs and the calves.

These exercises have to be specific. The ones I have outlined below should be part of your training routine. By developing specific muscles you will get to make much stronger and much higher jumps on the field.

The Exercises

- **Ab crunches**: 4-6 sets, for 15-20 repetitions
- **Spiderman Plank Crunch**: 4–6 reps, 10 reps for each side
- f: 3-4 sets, 1–2 minutes each
- **Jump** Squat: 4-6 sets, 10–12 reps each and one minute's rest between each set
- **Frog Jumps**: 4-6 sets, 10–12 reps each and one minute's rest between each set
- **Squats**: High rep range, low to moderate weights
- **Calves**: Do calf raises seated and raised, as well as leg presses on the smith machine (a piece of equipment used in weight training found in most commercial gyms around the country).

All of these exercises will help to improve your vertical jump and have you reaching heights you never thought possible.

However, jumping is only half the battle. You still need to know how to improve your headers and make them reach the net when that's the aim.

Here are four effective ways to help you improve your heading skills:

- **One**: Take a few steps toward the ball instead of waiting for it to come to you (a common mistake made by many). This will help you reach the ball before other players on the opposite team, as well as allowing you to create enough speed and propulsion to strike the ball forcefully with your head.
- **Two**: If you want to send the ball in the same direction as your run, use your forehead to strike it as opposed to the sides. Keep the ball in a straight line and maybe in a slightly upward direction. This will let you send a strong ball at a lethal height (mid-range and above). Shots like these, at the right speed and the right height, are very difficult for keepers to save.
- **Three**: If you want to send the ball in a direction other than the one you're running in, then lean forward and use the side of your head to strike it in the direction you want it to go. Striking the ball at a lethal angle from a header shot is far more effective than a powerful kick from the same angle. A good, successful header shot should combine both speed and direction. The one important thing to keep in mind with angled headers is to avoid directing the ball toward your body, i.e. your shoulder or your hands (this happens a lot).

- **Four**: When the goalkeeper looks as though he's in a good position to catch or save your ball, try to send him a bouncy header instead of a more direct one. Heading the ball towards the ground will change its direction and confuse him. The one thing you need to be mindful about with headers like these is to direct your ball towards the middle ground, which is the point between you and the goal. This is because the ball will lose its power if bounced before the middle area. Furthermore, it won't reach enough vertical bouncing height in order to trick the goalie if you bounce it too short of the middle point. He will also have more chance of saving your header if the ball bounces too far past the middle point, nearer his goal line. Therefore, in order to get the best results possible, you will have aim to bounce the ball right in the middle, just between you and the goalkeeper.

3. Failure to Improve the Power of Your Shots

If you want to truly become the best that you can possibly be, then you need the ability to send strong, accurate, and lethal, long shots at a moment's notice. Failing to improve the power of your kicks will come back to haunt you sooner rather than later.

Quite often, a young striker might think he's about as good as he can get, and the only thing remaining for him to do is maintain what he already has. This is often not the case. Unless you are preparing for retirement, there are always ways to improve in all areas of your game.

If you already have a powerful kick, then it's time to make it even more powerful. Never make the mistake of thinking you have nothing left to give because you have. I don't even have to know you to know this is true.

Ok, so it will require a lot of hard work, especially if you're already a well-developed player and looking to squeeze a bit more out of yourself, but you can still improve your shot accuracy and speed nonetheless, so don't let your mind or anyone else try to convince you otherwise.

Just like with improving your jumps, the power of your kick will require that you work out at a gym. Having access to all the right equipment will allow you to effectively build the required strength and body muscle that will enhance the power of your shots.

Don't forget, we're not just looking at improved power here, but accuracy (direction) as well. After all, it's no good having a super powerful kick that travels long distances off course.

Let's take a look the player in Europe who has the most powerful long balls right now, at the time of writing (2015). Actually, there are two of them, Swedish striker Zlatan Ibrahimović, and Brazilian forward, Givanildo Vieira de Sousa, aka Hulk.

OK, we'll look at each of these guys in turn and see what it is that makes them so special.

Both players are incredibly powerful, extremely well built, and tremendously brutal with their shots, so much so that they create fear for both goalkeepers and the defenders who face them whenever they go to strike the ball.

Earlier this year, while practicing with his team, Hulk (and there's probably a reason for calling him this) was simply preparing to play one of his "normal" shots. However, it seemed evident on this day that he was a little bit upset or fired-up for some reason ("you wouldn't like me when I'm angry."

Sorry, I just had to get that in). Hulk then struck the ball with all the might he could muster and... BAM!

The ball picked up the keeper as if it were a cannonball, sending the goalie through the back of his net leaving a huge hole in it. If you haven't seen this, and feel it's a little far-fetched, then you can check the video out if you want, just search for "Hulk, goalkeeper and net."

The Perfect Shot

If you search YouTube with the term "the best long shot goals in soccer" you will always find Ibrahimović and Ronaldo in just about every single video, and for good reason too.

Ibrahimović's goal against Anderlecht in the UEFA Champions League is one of the most impressive goals you will ever see in soccer. I highly recommend you go and watch it now.

Just type in Zlatan + Anderlecht and look for the one with the long shot, or better still, watch them all. They all make great, inspirational viewing, and that includes his amazing back-heel kick.

This long-shot goal is a demonstration of how power, when combined with accuracy, can mean disaster for the goalkeeper. With a shot like this, I really don't think the goalie could have reached the ball, not even if he was standing right in its path.

Being able to shoot like this, with such power and incredible accuracy, is the result of persistent and relentless training. Ibrahimović knew what he had to do in order to work on his skills and take his shooting (both short and long ranged) up to a whole new level, and so he followed through with his decision and got straight to work.

He developed his skills to the point where he has now become one of the best strikers in the last decade, and all this despite him being a bit short on both speed and mobility.

With a strong body and an immense power-shot, Ibrahimović made himself one of soccer's untouchable strikers.

It's a similar story with soccer superstar Ronaldo. Search for his goal with Man United against FC Porto in the 2009 Champions league. Once you watch this you will see exactly how far accuracy and a strong foot can take you.

Man United needed to score to qualify for the semi–finals after ending their first leg game with a 2–2 draw at the Old Trafford.

With a wonderful strike and a world class effort, Ronaldo managed to end it all and win his team the game (and later the championship) with his valuable skill of accuracy, long–shooting, and ability to score from a great distance.

When it comes to long shots, you must be confident that you are able to shoot accurately. Failure to do this would mean there's a good chance the opponents could intercept the ball mid-air as it goes astray.

Another important skill is having the ability to accurately shoot the ball straight away, the moment it reaches you, whether it approaches along the ground or in mid–air.

I see too many amateur attackers who fail to react properly with unexpected balls. This is especially the case when a ball arrives just a few centimeters above the ground. A lot of the time, an amateur striker would send his ball far above the goal, which is a waste of an otherwise good opportunity.

What Goalkeepers Fear the Most

No matter how brave or skilled they are, all goalkeepers fear for their safety when guarding their goal.

Not only are various saving techniques particularly risky, but that ball, and the boots that kick it, can sometimes move around a keeper like a frenzied beast, with all the power of a head-on locomotive, or at least that's' how it can appear in a fast moving, aggressive game.

There have also been a few nasty accidents in goal, and keepers know that these incidents can happen to them at any time. This is why they maintain a healthy fear when playing in goal, but they also need to be somewhat "fearless: too if they're to be any good. It's all about finding the right balance.

Look at the Czech goalie, Petr Čech. He's still wearing a protective head cover whenever he plays in goal. This is because he sustained a serious head injury in the game against Reading at the Madejski Stadium on 14 October 2006.

What happened was that Čech collided with midfielder Stephen Hunt inside Chelsea's penalty area within the first minute of the game. Thankfully he recovered, but doctors later reported that it nearly cost Čech his life.

So you're dealing with men (keepers) who fear for themselves even though they tend to be "fearless" in nature. Note that all keepers will fear some players more so than others, and the more they fear someone, the better chances those players have of defeating the goalie.

If you become known for having super powerful shots, then a goalie will naturally be a bit more cautious of you than he would with those who are more "average' with their strikes.

Whenever there's caution there will be an inevitable decline, to some degree, in the keeper's ability to save the shot. By the way, it's not only goalkeepers who will fear you.

Defenders will also move away from your powerful shots, or at the very least, they will treat you with more fear and less aggression, once you become a force to be reckoned with on the field.

No matter how much a player gets paid, he doesn't want to risk getting hit in the face by a flying missile or another player's boot, and certainly not to the point where his life is in danger, or he becomes disfigured in some way. He might love the game and be hungry to win, but not at the cost of serious injury.

Being all-powerful is an asset for any great striker to possess.

The Roberto Carlos Effect

I remember when Roberto Carlos used to play for Real Madrid. It was funny to watch whenever he would take a foul because the defenders creating the wall would literally panic.

Seriously, they would shrink their bodies like crazy, and sometimes jump out of fear, just in case Carlos' ball hit them at full force.

Carlos' fouls were stunning to watch. He would stay away from the ball, and then sprint 10 or 20 meters before sending an extremely strong shot toward the goal.

Quite often the ball would reach the goal simply because the guys in the defensive wall were too afraid to stay put. It was hilarious to watch as they'd jump up and let the speeding ball pass under them.

His foul against France in 1998 is the fastest and strongest foul shots ever recorded, both in the history of old and modern soccer. The man is a true legend.

Ask anybody who's ever played Winning Eleven on Play Station One, and they'll tell you that whenever they needed a goal, everybody would place

Carlos on the right wing (instead of the right back), and use his speed and power to score tons of guaranteed goals. He was a legend for a whole generation, and quite rightly so.

For your shots to be incredibly powerful you will have to make sure of the following:

- **One**: Tighten your core (abs). This is to make sure you are transmitting enough power from your body to the ball. Think of it like collecting energy before an explosion.
- **Two**: Ensure there is enough controlled movement with your leg (the one that will make the kick) so that you have enough energy to strike the ball.
- **Three**: Perform explosive one leg lunges. Simply take the one leg lunge position, and then when you're coming up, kick with your knee as if you're striking someone it. This will increase the explosive action of your knees when kicking the ball, thus allowing you to quickly launch your powerful shot.

- **Four**: You must die for every single ball and expect to score from every single opportunity that comes your way. Anyone who tells you other than this is either lying to you or has a different agenda. The greatest strikers in the world of soccer are those who treat every play and every ball as if it's a game winner.

Look around you and ask yourself who the best strikers in the world are right now. As far as European clubs are concerned, it has to be Ronaldo, Messi, Zlatan, Kun Agüero and Luis Suarez.

I will use Luis Suarez as an example.

The Uruguayan striker is not only considered by many soccer fans to be one of the best five strikers in the entire world right now, but he's also thought by many to be one of the best attackers in the history of the English premier league.

I believe the main reason behind Suarez's massive success is his relentless attacks on every single ball and every single play.

He is super tenacious in his approach to succeed at every opportunity, even when the odds look as though they're stacked against him.

But don't take my word for it, simply hit YouTube and look for a video for his goal against Juventus in the UEFA Champions league final, and you will see a perfect example of his style of play.

It was a counter attack for Barcelona against Juventus, when Neymar sent the ball towards Gianluigi Buffon's goal, but Buffon's successfully deflected the ball away. However, Suarez then made a rapid follow up and sent the ball straight to the empty net.

Recently I saw a video on one of the websites that covers soccer stats and analysis. They had been monitoring the movement of every single Barcelona player throughout an entire game.

This particular video focused specifically on Suarez and his movements on the field while play with on.

When you watch the game, or look at the goal for the first time, you will think it was a simple follow up shot.

However, all is not as it seems. When your watch the goal more carefully, you realize that Suarez moves toward the far post (the very place the ball deflected to after Buffon played it) even before Neymar took the shot.

4. Not Fighting for Every Ball

Play on every ball a defender is passing, heading or receiving, and always expect him to make mistakes, so that if and when they actually do happen, you're ready to go in for the kill and take a shot at the goal.

Defenders have their moments when they lose focus and make silly mistakes, and this goes for goalkeepers too. Your job is to apply pressure and expect these slipups to happen because they will, sometimes.

Whether you realize it or not, all goals are scored as a result of individual mistakes, like a wrong pass, a lack of communication between defenders and the keeper, a mistake in setting the offside trap, a weak positioning from the goal keeper, and so on and so forth.

Highly physical games require a special type of player, and anyone who follows soccer passionately will know who these guys are.

English fans just love to see highly skilled players like Messi and Neymar perform their magic on the field, maneuvers like dribbling through four or five players before finally scoring, and other moves that simply send the crowds into a state of frenzied delight.

I have watched Luis Suarez long before he signed up for Liverpool and then later Barcelona. I can remember watching him begin to shine in the days when he played for Ajax Amsterdam, before 2012.

I can tell you that nobody can succeed in an extremely challenging, highly physical competition, like the English premier league, unless they have that special something.

Here you have teams like Stoke City, Birmingham City, Blackburn Rovers, West Ham United and Bolton, all of who play very physical games and build their strategy on solid defensive techniques and rough play.

This kind of physical roughness requires a player who doesn't tire easily, plays on every ball, and gives his opponents a hard time for the entire duration of a game, and in all weathers too. Believe me when I say the British weather can throw some pretty rough days at you, in any season.

Ever heard of Joey Barton or Vinnie Jones? If not, you will know who they are in a moment, and why I'm mentioning them.

Joey Barton plays as midfielder for Queens Park Rangers in England. He is perhaps one of the dirtiest players you will ever see in your entire life.

In fact, he is only second, after Lee Catermole (midfielder for Sunderland), to receive the most red cards in the history of the premier league. Playing against Barton is quite easy, although it does requires a special approach and a lot of patience.

Barton will grab your shirt, hit you in sensitive places, punch you in the face while jumping (so that it appears like an accident), tackle you badly in a known weak foot, or simply give you a knock out in front of the referee.

It's clearly evident that Barton doesn't care about anyone but himself. He once shoved a cigar into the eye of another player during a training session because something or other upset him.

Now onto Vinnie Jones, the former professional soccer player (midfielder from 1984 to 1999, notably for Wimbledon, Leeds United, Sheffield United and Chelsea,) now turned actor. Jones was infamous for what his fans called "Jones' first warning" where he would give you a difficult time from the outset.

His typical tactic was to go in hard, very hard, usually by giving you a really tough tackle at the beginning of the game, almost as if to warn you of what to expect if you dared to get in his way again.

What you need to know is that defenders who play like these two guys, in a crazy, highly aggressive manner, is actually a gift to you. Yes, I did say a gift.

These types of players are easily upset and become stressed at the slightest thing. What this means is that they are also prone to losing their focus real easy too. You just can't be in an agitated state of mind and hold good focus, the two just don't mix.

Therefore, it's in your best interest to get guys like Joey Barton and Vinnie Jones hot and bothered. The good news is that you don't have to stoop to their unsportsmanlike levels to achieve this.

All you have to do as a way to upset these field bullies is play a better game than they do. That's it in a nutshell.

Any soccer player outsmarted by an opponent finds it frustrating, yet most will soon recover and move on with their game.

For players who can't handle defeat too well, getting beat in a tackle, or outsmarted in a particular play, often gets them agitated and sees them lose some focus. Therefore, being the better player is your secret weapon against the field intimidators.

Giving them a hard time by being the more composed player (and this is what Suarez used to do with players of this type) will either allow you to score a goal more easily or get the bully sent off. Whichever scenario occurs creates a win-win situation for you either way.

Mess with the Man Marking You

Messing with the other team's defenders has nothing to do with foul play, it simply means you keep them under pressure and don't allow them a second to relax or time to recompose.

You're playing a good mental game when you can keep the pressure on your opponents, which can be just as effective as the physical game. Zlatan Ibrahimović was an expert at messing with the opposition's defenders.

I have yet to see any player better than Ibrahimović at keeping his opponents distracted and out of their game.

Others often see his confidence as cockiness and arrogance, or the result of an inflated ego, which is probably true to some extent.

Anyway, the Swedish striker just loves to play mind games with the defender who's marking him, and he does an excellent job at it too.

Ibrahimović would gain an edge by simply intimidating the other defenders. He would mess with their confidence, trying to make them feel "less than" or get them angry or aggressive with him.

Any or all of these things eventually work to serve Ibrahimović's purpose. He knows that whenever an opponent takes his bait, that player loses some of his focus, which in turn affects his ability to play well.

I can recall one incident in a game where Ibrahimović was playing with Paris Saint-Germain against AS Saint-Etienne in the French league. The incident occurred when one of Saint–Etienne's defenders was aggressively marking Ibrahimović during a corner kick. Actually, the man was only doing his job, but unlucky for him, Ibrahimović didn't like that and decided to do something about it.

What happened next was that Ibrahimović kept bugging him throughout the rest of the game, knowing that he had to break him. He kept looking at the back of his t–shirt, trying to pronounce his name in a mocking way. He would taunt him further by looking him straight in the eye, provoking him with his criticisms.

Well, it finally worked. Ibrahimović's opponent totally lost his focus and became more of a liability to his side than a help. Once Ibrahimović had achieved his objective, he then went on to score with very little serious challenge from the now broken defender.

You might feel that playing this way is no better that the physical bullying of players like Joey Barton and Vinnie Jones, but it's not.

As long as you're only being verbally provocative and not verbally abusive, or obstructing the defender's way by blocking him when he doesn't have the ball, then you are simply playing a good mental game.

How the other player responds is not your business. If he can't block you out and get on with his game unaffected, then he needs to make some personal improvements in this area because this kind of mental tactic is rife in modern soccer.

How effective it is depends on the mental skills of the one doing the taunting and the ability of the taunted one to block you out.

Another technique that is worth mentioning is to use any kind of successful tactic that worked previously against a team, or a certain keeper or defender, which gave you results the previous time you played against them.

We often reflect on what went wrong during a game so that we can improve our future performance, but it's equally as important to chalk up what went right too. Looking at all aspects of your play, good, bad, or neutral, is what will turn you into a well-rounded player.

It's also worth learning how to be a little unpredictable as well. As you know, before a game a well-prepared team will study their rivals as best they can so that they can be better prepared for the day.

If a player is totally predictable in the way he plays, then the opposing side will probably be prepared for that, and therefore know how to deal with him accordingly.

Some predicable qualities, however, are worth keeping. For example, if you become well-known for something that you excel in particularly well, like a hard legal tackle, or your ability to get others riled with your provocative, close-up-and-personal banter, then there's a good chance that your opponents will fear you more, and whenever there's fear, or apprehension, things can work in your favor.

To begin with, throwing doubt in the other player's minds may result in them getting a little overly aggressive because of nerves and a determination to beat you. When this happens, they are more at risk of making fouls and getting yellow or red cards because of it.

They are also more likely to make silly blunders when they're fearful of you. Neither of these things would have occurred if your presence on the field hadn't intimidated them mentally.

Something else worth noting is that whenever defenders start to get cautious or nervous around you and start to close in, they are actually helping you create space for the second striker playing near you.

This is great since it will leave him without proper marking, which will make his life easier too, giving him more opportunities to score than he would have otherwise had.

5. Shooting When Having No Chance to Score

Keep it smart when shooting. This means knowing when to shoot and when to hold back. Avoid sending balls that you know 100% have no chance of reaching the goal.

This is especially evident when shooting from a dead angle on when shooting through the crowd. In cases like these it's better to be creative.

Either pass the ball on to a better positioned teammate or find yourself another solution rather than risk losing the ball.

Some players wait until the last few minutes of a game and then start to shoot from everywhere in the general direction of the goal. They also start shouting at the referee and trying to look super angry and intensely involved in the game.

This typically happens with players who know they've underperformed throughout the competition. What they're doing is trying to make a last minute impression with the fans. They do this hoping to escape criticism for being lazy or letting down the side. Fans are not that stupid, of course!

The English team, Wigan Athletic, once had a player who did those types of things. In general he played pretty well, but when he had an off day he was full of hot air. He was an Egyptian and his name was Amr Zaki.

This guy's case was weird. Zaki was on loan to Wigan in the summer of 2008 from the Egyptian league. Within his first 13 games he had scored 10 goals.

One of his goals was a spectacular bicycle kick against Liverpool. Within just a few months other teams began to send their scouts to track his performance.

Anyway, the point is this. Not every game will be your game. You can't leave every competition with a victory and get to bask in egotistical glory.

If your team happens to be losing to a better side on the day, just continue to play the best game you can.

No one can expect more from you than that. Whatever you do don't begin to exaggerate everything and take wild shots just to look good. If you do, then the fans, your teammates, and your coach will see right through you.

If you know a kick will get blocked, don't perform it. Playing safe will give you much more potential than potluck ever could.

6. Don't Settle for Second Best

Every great team is based on four key players; a strong goal keeper, a solid center back, a tough defender/midfielder and a 30 goal per season striker.

Give any coach these four players and he can work miracles. In fact, during his late days in Man United (the days after Ronaldo had moved to Real Madrid), Sir Alex Ferguson managed to win league titles with a group of average, and sometimes below average or mediocre even, players.

The reason he accomplished this was because he had Edwin Van der Sar (GK), Rio Ferdinand and Vidić (CB), Michael Carrick (DM) and Ruud van Nistelrooy along with Wayne Rooney.

Why I'm mentioning all this?

Because I want you to realize that A–class strikers are both rare and invaluable. Big teams can, and quite often do, pay big bucks for these guys.

Anyone can judge a team's performance and its ability to win trophies and championships by knowing who plays on that team's front line.

Ordinary and average teams have ordinary and average strikers. Even if they do manage to get an exceptional striker every now and again, chances are he won't be around for too long before some other club snaps him up by offering a much better deal.

Mediocre goals lead to mediocre actions and eventually a mediocre soccer experience.

Never settle for second best. Don't let anyone, including you, tell yourself that you are about as good as you're ever likely to get. If you do, then you won't move on because you will become, or remain, what you have accepted as your best.

Instead, you should aim as high as your imagination can take you. Set goals bigger than you can envisage and have very high expectations of yourself.

As long as the mini-goals, the ones leading up to the main objective, are achievable, then the sky really is the limit.

If you tell yourself you can't do a thing then you're right, you can't. If you tell yourself you can do a thing, then there's a good chance you will achieve your objectives. No great player has got to where is by disbelieving in himself.

Setting big goals, and believing they're possible, is the only way you will get to reach your true potential. Anything less and you will plod on as just another Joe Average player, wishing you could have been more like others.

You're probably wondering how you can instill a strong belief system into your psyche. Well, this is where I introduce you to "The 10X Rule".

This has to be one of the best books ever written about success and having a winning mindset. The 10X Rule is a book by an American Multimillionaire salesman called Grant Cardone.

I have read this book cover to cover many times in the past and will continue to re-read it. I highly recommend that you do the same.

Don't worry, this isn't just another self-help book from some self-confessed inspirational coach, it really is a motivational and practical program for success.

Grant Cardone will teach you the real principles of self-belief. Seriously, if you need a boost of motivation, a fresh approach that will inspire you to raise your standards so that you can achieve still higher goals, then this is the only book you will ever need.

I recommend that you read and reread this book until the principles of the 10X Rule embed deep inside your mind.

When this happens, the way you think, feel, and function will change forever, and change for the better.

Honestly, once you have read it through once or twice, you will come to realize why so many people call this book the encyclopedia of success.

Any great soccer player has to develop his mindset in order to excel in his position, and the 10X Rule can help you to do just that.

If you would like to have the same winning attitude and outlook as players like Cristiano Ronaldo and Wayne Rooney, just know that you now have an invaluable tool at your disposal that will surely help you to really achieve your objectives and remove any self-doubts that you may have previous had.

Let me tell you something about the Grant Cardone approach as a way to give you a flavor of his teaching.

The main and most important methodology in this book is the idea of aiming high.

You start this this by setting huge, extremely big goals, usually way beyond the targets you had previously set for yourself.

Now you might already be thinking that this is an unrealistic approach draped in fantasy, especially as I always talk about the importance of setting "realistic" goals in my books. However, when I talk of being "realistic," I am usually referring to the mini goals, or checkpoints, used as stepping stones to the end target, and not the main goal, which should always be set high.

Having very ambitious goals will push and motivate you toward taking more actions and achieving more results.

That sounds logical, obviously, but the problem is that so many of us never aim high enough, and that restricts us from realizing our full potential.

Whether we know it or not, we all have self-doubt, to a greater or lesser degree, and it's only when we release ourselves from the shackles of this curse that we are able to excel beyond our wildest dreams. This is where the 10X Rule comes to your rescue.

In this book, the author suggests that whenever you're planning to achieve a certain goal you must make that goal 10, 20 or even 50 times bigger than the one you had previously set, or plan to set for yourself.

Grant Cardone also advocates using smaller, more achievable goals as a way to reach your main objective, just as I have done in my guides.

This is a logical and very workable approach. Because your end goal is now much bigger, you will naturally be keen to get there as soon as you can.

This means your mini goals will also be more ambitious, and so your efforts will naturally intensify. Small, mediocre, easily achieved goals, on the other hand, will result in mediocre progress and block your ability to excel.

OK, let's use an entrepreneurial scenario as a way to illustrate these points.

Imagine that you want to build a new company for yourself and that your main objective is to generate a decent income.

Which would you prefer to end up with for your efforts, a company worth $500,000 dollars or $100,000,000 million dollars?

It doesn't take a genius to answer a successful $100,000,000 dollar company would be the most preferable outcome.

If you set yourself a goal to make a 100 million dollar company, you would naturally be in a different mindset and therefore take on a different approach for the entire venture.

Chances are you would be more aggressive, more ambitious and driven than you would be if you had settled on creating a company worth $500,000 dollars.

Here's something to think about: If you set yourself a lower goal, then it is highly unlikely that you will ever exceed it. Put another way, if you believe you are only able to achieve something up to a certain level, you are absolutely right.

Most people only "dream" about doing great things, or becoming what others have become, and that's usually where it stops, at the dreaming stage. In other words, they only fantasize about greatness, but they don't believe it could ever happen to them, and so it never does.

Whenever someone doesn't believe they can become much greater than they are, that doesn't mean they can't, it just means they think they can't, and they're right, they can't, at least not when they put such restrictions on themselves. This is why they have to unleash their real potential, and the only way to do that is to change their belief system.

Any of the great soccer strikers will tell you that they set themselves high goals when they were developing their skills.

The only reason they could aim high was because they genuinely believed they could get to where they wanted to go, even though they were a long way off from that place as young, enthusiastic players.

If they didn't believe, then they would never have made the grade. If you want to be up there with the world's best strikers, then that has to be your end goal. Anything less and you will fall short.

The next time you're playing with your team, set a higher standard for yourself and aim to score a hat-trick or even a super hat-trick, instead of just playing it small and hoping you'll do well on the day.

Take this "higher goal" approach in everything that you do, and that includes training session as well.

Always strive to excel beyond anything you have hoped for in the past. Maintain your focus and never settle for anything less than greatness. Don't worry if you fall short, because you will do, and on numerous occasions, but the point is to learn from any failures and never ever lower the bar.

Aim high, and continue to aim high and great things will materialize as long as you believe they will. Remember to never let any setbacks influence you in a negative way, just shrug them off as mere blips along the way and keep moving forward.

A winning mentality is what creates winners, and so this is to be your mindset. This is the way of thinking and believing that you need to hardwire into your psyche.

This is how big teams win big games and big trophies. For example, look at a dominant team like Bayern Munich, and a dominant coach like Guardiola.

They enter each game with the aim of coming away with more than just three points. They are always hungry for more and always wanting to score 7-8 goals per game.

In fact, Bayern Munich is the only team in Europe to have the highest number of goals scored per game, and without having star players like the goal scoring machines Messi and Ronaldo on their side.

Only you can determine your success. You have to fall in love with the dream and give it the required effort to turn it into a reality.

When you get to change the way you view yourself and your potential, then positive changes will become inevitable.

7. Not Properly
Positioning Yourself

The king of positioning was perhaps the retired Italian striker, Filippo Inzaghi.

Inzaghi was one of the most underrated strikers of the last decade. The Milanista spent his first two years playing for Juventus before becoming one of AC Milan's icons of all times. He had two league cups and two champions league titles during his 11 years with AC Milan (2001–2012).

Inzaghi (who got sacked from coaching Milan in 2015), scored 126 goals in 300 games for the club when he played for them as a striker.

I have seen all his goals in a single video, and only two of them were from outside the penalty area. In fact, even the two goals from outside the penalty area came about as a result of one-to-one situations where Inzaghi kicked the ball just a few inches outside the penalty box.

However, the rest of his goals - and here's the brilliance - came about by positioning himself in perfect spots from where he got to increase his opportunities for scoring easy goals from within the penalty area.

Inzaghi wasn't the best among his peers, not even close. He wasn't as skilled as Ronaldo, he wasn't lethal like his other teammate, Ukrainian Andriy Shevchenko, and he wasn't as strong as the Argentine, Gabriel Batistuta, who was the best league striker at that time.

Despite being short on skills and in his physical attributes, Inzaghi was by far the smartest among his peers, not just in Italy but in Europe as well. This was because of his adherence to his tactical game.

Always Stay Near the Goal.

The most important skill you should have as a striker is to get as close to the goal as much as possible, even though it might cause you to be offside on occasions. This skill becomes even more important when you're not physically that strong, and especially as you become an older player.

In fact, one of the tactical skills that Inzaghi exploited like no other player, in Italy and wider Europe, was to continuously throw himself into the offside.

I know, this might sound crazy (it looks crazy to me actually), but when you really think about it, you will know that he was right in his decisions most of the time.

Strikers like Inzaghi feed on deflected balls, goalkeeper mistakes, and erratic balls from the keeper or the defense.

You can see these guys saving their energy, waiting for the right moments, and once they come, as they always do, BAM! They move in fast and score.

Think of it this way: keeping yourself close to the goal, and the last of the other team's defensive players, puts you in a good spot tactically.

Furthermore, if you keep testing the lineman's accuracy in spotting you in the offside, then you will have at least a couple of good chances throughout the game to catch a breakaway, and therefore pose as a real threat for the other team.

You should also get a couple of opportunities to score too, once you've developed a good system for yourself.

Inzaghi thought, and correctly so as it turned out, that all he needed was one successful breakaway out of 10 in order to create an easy chance for him, or for his teammates, to score a goal.

Anyone who can score one or more goals per game, or even one goal every two games, will become one of the top scoring players on their team, if not the top scorer.

One of Inzaghi's greatest moments ever was when he scored two goals against Liverpool in the 2007 UEFA Champions league final. In this particular game, he helped AC Milan win by 2–1. If you saw that game live or have watched it on YouTube, you would have seen the pure brilliance of the man at work in both of his goals.

In the first goal, he placed himself in the path of Andrea Pirlo's foul that was close to the penalty area. Here he deflected the ball towards the net. The second goal was a complete demonstration of Inzaghi's offside skills.

He received a through pass from Kaka, and just at that time he managed to beat the offside trap as well as the four Liverpool defenders who were surrounding him.

With only one move at his disposal, he managed to get himself in a one-to-one situation with Liverpool's goalkeeper, Pepe Reina, but he didn't have any trouble moving around him and scoring his second goal of the game.

Inzaghi was smart, and his way of thinking made him one of the living legends of AC Milan. Believe me, in the world of competitive soccer there can be no greater honor than that.

If you can fall in love with the near post you will excel. Take it from someone who has seen a lot in his time. Falling in love with that near post is something that all smart players learn to do, sooner or later.

This is in fact a most basic skill, albeit one of the trickiest for any striker to master well.

The idea is to simply wait for the right moment, and then, when all the other team's defenders are busy watching the ball or marking your teammates, you get yourself over to the near post, anticipating a touch on the ball and scoring a goal, either with your head or your foot.

This skill of waiting at the near post to snatch some goals was also one of Inzaghi`s greatest attributes. Since he wasn`t super tall (only 1.81m) he would find it better not to compete with defenders who were taller than himself.

He would choose to leave them marking other teammates, hide himself within the crowd, and when the right moment came along he would score, nice and easy.

Another example is the two Spanish stars who have won everything with Barcelona. I am of course referring to the forward or winger Pedro Rodriguez, and striker David Villa.

Though both Rodriguez (1.69m) and Villa (1.75m) are two of the shortest attacking players in Europe, both of them still managed to compensate for the loss in centimeters with speed and vision.

Their unique abilities enabled them to win the Spanish Liga and the Champions league as well as the FIFA Club world cup.

Both of these players have managed to leave their mark at Barcelona, despite competing with other great players in the attacking line, like Thierry Henry, Samuel Eto'o, and of course Lionel Messi.

The point I'm making here is that even if you fall short in height, that doesn't mean you have to fail. If you are not tall enough, then you have to compensate with other skills.

This is the only way to excel and keep scoring despite any competition you may face, but it is possible for anyone who's determined enough.

8. Not Knowing How to Run

Another thing for you to keep in mind when trying to beat the offside trap is to run diagonally or sideways as you prepare for your teammates to pass the ball to you.

By doing this, you are running to escape the defender marking you and to find a clearer space for yourself.

Here you're making your runs a bit longer, gaining some seconds before your teammate (who's probably being marked) finds the right opportunity to pass you the ball.

This is a better approach than running directly in a straight line, which also risks you putting yourself in the offside.

However, this approach can only be done when you receive a "straight" ball, but if your teammate decides to send you a diagonal pass that goes through the other team`s defense, then you will have to run as fast as you can in a straight line to reach the ball before any other player gets to it.

A straight pass will occur mostly when there are a very few defenders playing against you and you`re trying to escape the offside. A diagonal pass will occur mostly via a through-pass, sent through a number of other players.

The Way to Get Rid of Isolation or Trapping

Speed is by far the best way for you to escape from being isolated on the other side of the field. In some games you will find yourself suddenly isolated and your team outnumbered at the front.

In these situations, you will have nobody to assist you, especially when you`re playing a defensive game against a stronger team, or when your team is playing with 10 or less players because one of your teammates has been sent off with a red card.

The way out of these situations is to move around a lot and look for the ball. Move to the middle so that you can receive early passes from your midfielders who can`t reach out to you at the front.

This style of play will require you to be physically very fit as you will need to cover large areas throughout the entire game.

It will also necessitate some leadership and self-reliance skills since you`ll be doing everything with minimum support from the other players.

You need to make intelligent runs off the ball to disrupt the opponent`s defense and formation. You can also offer help to other attacking teammates who are playing close to you, or assist any other player in your team by your smart, well–timed runs.

The idea is to simply make the opposition defenders follow you, and thus move pressure away from your teammates.

Once you get good at anticipating a pass before the defense you'll always maintain the upper hand. With a continuous state of motion, combined with enough physical strength and smart positioning, you will definitely get to steal a lot of balls, airborne or on the ground, before the defensive players near to you can get to them.

Yes, this way of playing can be extremely exhausting and requires much work at the gym and extra effort at training sessions in order to reach such levels of peak fitness.

Even so, providing you want it enough then you won't have any problem reaching such levels of mobility and endurance. For ambitious players, hard work is all par for the course and the price that has to be paid in order to become great at the job.

Soccer is a serious business alright, but it should also be about enjoyment, in fact, you won't find any successful player who doesn't love what he does. He simply wouldn't be able to perform at his peak if he wasn't in love with the game.

If it wasn`t hard, then everyone would be "great," and no one would shine above all others. Thankfully, it's not like that, and nor would the ambitious types want it to be easy. After all, competitiveness is in their blood so they need to compete.

9. Failing to Let Go of past Mistakes

To illustrate the problem with failing to let go of past mistakes we will look at a case study.

The Rise and Fall of Torres

Soccer lovers and fans the world over have mixed opinions of the Spanish striker Fernando Torres. Many of them think of him as an attacking legend, not least because of his early, outstanding performance with both Atletico Madrid and Liverpool.

Others view him in a totally different light, seeing him more as a flop than a hit, especially because of his unexpected, weak performance with both Chelsea and AC Milan.

In fact, nobody knows quite what happened to Fernando Torres that changed him from a £50 million striker (the most expensive center forward at that time) to the Joe Average Torres he has become today.

The only thing I can think of that has caused his performance to decline so dramatically is self-doubt. Any player will tell you that once confidence is lost it can become incredibly difficult to regain

In his heyday, Torres was fantastic, outstanding and quite lethal. He was the best striker in the World, a World Cup winner and a UEFA winner with Spain. He was able to do anything with the ball, scoring, creating assists, playing fouls, in fact, you name it he did it. He was complete.

Torres scored 91 goals for Atletico before surpassing all expectations at Liverpool with 72 goals in his first three seasons with the club (almost 25 goals per season).

He then went on to play for Chelsea for a record breaking £50 million, making him the fourth most expensive signing in world soccer, behind Cristiano Ronaldo, Zlatan Ibrahimović and Kaka.

For Chelsea this was a very significant day as they had captured one of the best players in the world with his best years still ahead of him, or so they thought. Let's look at his time with Chelsea, the professional English soccer club based in Fulham F.C, London.

The Chelsea Era

Soon after joining Chelsea, it looked as if Torres had lost it all. He lost his magic touch and wasted easy goals; even when the goals were empty he missed! He even failed to score during his first few games at the club.

It looked as though the huge pressure bestowed on Fernando Torres, not only by Chelsea fans, but also by the English media along with the entire soccer world, was affecting his performance big time.

That £50 Million deal was an unexpected move from Chelsea and obviously attracted massive attention at the time. With that attention came huge pressure for the talented striker, pressure, it seems, that was just too much too bear.

His performance went from bad to worse with each game he failed to score in. He finished his first season with Chelsea scoring just one goal from 18 games. After that, he went on to score 11 goals in 49 games.

Torres' performance kept declining and before long he found himself loaned out to AC Milan (AC Milan was out of budget and was only in a position to buy cheap or out of contract players at the time).

What happened to Torres exactly, and what caused his performance to decline so drastically in such a short space of time? Well, people had mixed views on this. Some thought it was a result of Chelsea`s defensive style.

Others say it was because he had always been the solo striker for every team he'd played for before Chelsea, and so he couldn`t manage to play alongside another striker, as was expected of him at Chelsea FC.

I believe the reason for his sudden decline was twofold. Firstly, he lost his hunger, or passion for the game (something that appeared obvious by the way he approached each competition), and secondly, he lost that loyalty or responsibility that a "team" player must have.

Because of these things he surrendered to self-doubt. In other words, Torres' had let go of his mental game and his focus was lost because of it.

Whenever a player loses focus like this, determination, loyalty, and a genuine hunger for victory, all go out the window. It doesn't matter what physical talent he has, if his mind and body are on different pages, then there is no chance of playing at his optimum level.

In short, if the player doesn't want to do something, even though he knows he must, if his mind is in the wrong place then nothing or nobody can make him change other than himself.

As you can see, even one of the most talented players in the world can lose it all when his mind changes direction. Each failure to perform well in a game will negatively reinforce self-doubt still further.

The more a player fails to shine, the more he expects to underperform, and so the precedent is set for less as opposed to more.

The only way out of this quagmire is to retake control of the mind; something that is often easier said than done. Moreover, it will be harder for a player to regain that lost confidence the longer his decline goes on for.

In the case of Torres, his biggest mistake was to allow the media attention and extreme pressure to get to him. Being overly sensitive to expectations and criticism is what forced him to change for the worse.

Zooming in on all that negative attention made him lose focus (zoom out) on what was really important, which was to play the best game he could possibly play in each game. In other words, he had lost the ability to live in the now.

The Universal Mindset

Allowing ourselves to be influenced by external distractions is not only something that affects soccer players or sportspeople more generally. This is something that can, and often does, affect everyone, from all walks of life, to a greater or lesser degree, although we often don't know it.

The reason this happens is because a past, negative event, is rarely forgotten and the more we dwell on it the more it influences our mental state of mind.

Let's say, for example, you used to easily jump over a three foot wall, then one day, for some reason, you didn't clear that wall and you fell face down on the other side, banged your head really hard, and got some nasty grazes on your arms.

Even though you may have jumped over that wall successfully a thousand times before, you suddenly become reluctant, afraid that you might stumble again and sufferer the awful hurt of the previous leap.

You know you can clear the wall easily, after all, you've done it plenty of times before, but now you're not quite so confident, yet you decide to try again in a few days' time regardless of a little self-doubt.

When the day comes, and you have had time to lick your wounds, you approach the same wall with a little hesitancy this time, slightly afraid even, and unable to get that previous accident out of your head.

In this case, you have already set yourself up for potential failure. Let's say you clip the wall with one of your feet and BANG! Down you go again.

You've now increased your self-doubt and you may or may not attempt a third jump, or at least not right away.

This kind of past tense focus is a big trap for anyone to fall into, and this is what most probably happened to striker Torres when he moved over to Chelsea.

He got off to a bad start and found it hard to recover. He could feel that all eyes were upon him, and the more he failed to deliver, the less likely he became to succeed.

If, on the other hand, he had gotten off to a great start at Chelsea FC, then the opposite would have most likely happened as he would have fueled his brain with more positive-reinforcement as opposed to negative-reinforcement.

The best way to avoid these negative mind traps is to know about them. Once you understand why they're happening, and then put everything into a balanced perspective before it gets chance to take a hold, the better your chances are of avoiding this behavioral shift. Let's look at how to evade this paralyzing behavior.

One: Dwelling on your past successes won`t make you hungry for more.

Ask yourself what made the former Welsh soccer star Ryan Gigs (the most decorated player in English soccer history) keep playing with the same hunger and the same tenacity since he was 17 years old, right up until he retired at the age of 40.

This is a man who won everything with Man United, including 13 premier league titles and two Champions league cups.

Giggs has more league medals than the league titles like Chelsea (for the record Chelsea has five league titles). Yet despite all that, the man kept grounded and never once fazed. Giggs continued to amaze with his wonderful performance right up until his last game in 2014.

Let's look at another great performer, this time Cristiano Ronaldo. Ronaldo keeps scoring goals and breaking one record after the other, and this is despite having it all and achieving just about everything a soccer player could possibly dream of achieving in his career.

There's also Lionel Messi. What makes a player like Messi (already with four Ballon D`ors before reaching the age of 27) keep going the way he does, with relentless persistence?

The answer to these questions is simple. They never dwell on the past. Their focus is always on the present, looking at what they can do in the here-and-now.

They may revisit the past to learn from previous mistakes or to look at successful moments so that they can improve or maintain their current ability, but they NEVER allow themselves to dwell on the past, ever, nor do they beat themselves up by replaying any poor performances back in their minds as some kind of punishment after a game.

In fact, players like this look at any failure as "success in progress" rather than a setback. To them, failure is not fatal; it's merely an opportunity to learn from so that they can move on to greater things.

Whenever a player allows past mistakes to haunt him, he's on a downward spiral. This is especially true if he felt humiliation and shame at the time.

Have you ever heard the saying "it's like water off a ducks back?" It simply implies something doesn't upset you or that it doesn't "stick" in your mind. This is the kind of approach you need to adopt if you are to excel in the world of soccer.

You need to grow a thick skin and casually shrug off any blunders or underperformance and simply move on with your game, keeping your focus tight and in the present.

Once you get to develop the right mindset, then, and only then, are you able to set yourself more ambitious goals and maintain that hunger for the game. You have an unquenchable desire to conquer come rain, come shine, come hell or high water.

Nothing or nobody will affect you because you live in the here-and-now, and so your focus in on the moment, not what's already passed. This is the winning mentality.

Two: Focusing negatively on the past will trap you into a cycle of self-blaming.

Wasting a penalty, losing a duel, or even scoring an own goal, are not the kind of things that any player wants to experience although most players do, at some point, that's just a fact.

However, it is when such events make the player lose his focus that they become much bigger deals than the events themselves.

Getting over blunders on the field is not rocket science. The trick is to simply focus on the now, in other words, focus on your next move, your next pass, your next play and your next goal, shutting out all else from your mind than the game in hand.

That's it!

Puffing, tutting, getting embarrassed, reminiscing over what's just happened, or didn't happen, as they case may be, will hurt, not help, your performance and consequently, that of your team.

Knowing this, and accepting it, will allow you to develop and excel. The only good things to come out of past events are valuable lessons from which you get to learn from, thus helping you to grow into a stronger person and a better player.

Letting go means you have realized that some incident is now part of your history and not a part of your destiny. The game moves on and so should you. It's the only way to progress.

All you need to really know is this: living in the moment and keeping your head in the here-and-now, along with what needs doing in the very near future, will keep you motivated.

It will mean you'll be able to use your full mental and physical capacity and consequently score more goals. Anytime you're thinking about the past, you can't possibly be thinking about the present.

Never allow your past to mess with your present or your future plans and expectations. If you do, you will lose focus, confidence and motivation.

Once you take away whatever lesson needs taking from a previous experience, always throw the past behind you and return your focus so that you're back in the moment.

Once you can do this you will be able to recover from setbacks much easier, and in a short space-time.

Training your mind is no different to training your physical body in that the more you practice at it, the better and more natural things will become.

10. Failing to Take the Game Seriously

Case study: Mario Balotelli

The 25 year old Italian striker Mario Balotelli, is one of the best young talents in Europe and the world. At 1.89m he`s tall, and he's also strong, very strong, with a great set of shooting skills. He`s also one of the best penalty takers soccer has ever seen.

However, there is a problem with this star player in that he's too flippant in his approach and fails to take the game seriously. So even though he's great, he could be greater still if only he used his brain more.

Balotelli is probably one of the most immature player you will ever see playing professional soccer. He`s not disciplined at all, he gets angry quite easily, he`s extremely selfish, and he lacks proper direction.

He doesn`t even go to all the team's practice sessions. Balotelli is one of those players who seem to attract problems like bees to a honeypot.

Because of this, Balotelli has failed to make any real name for himself, except that is, for being a troublemaker. He's played for clubs all players of his age dream of playing for, like AC Milan, Manchester City, and Liverpool. No matter where he goes, he keeps making trouble and upsetting the flow of things.

It seems as though he`s taking his talent and his career with some disdain.

Other talented players of a similar age are achieving more trophies than him and breaking various records, yet these are things that Balotelli could easily smash if only he kept his focus and unleashed the great player that is undoubtedly there inside him. Alas, at the time of writing he shows no sign of changing his ways anytime soon.

As a matter of fact, his performance is dramatically declining (he scored just 4 goals in 28 games for Liverpool in 2014-15). Ask any coach in Europe if he would like to sign Balotelli and he will reply with an emphatic "NEVER". Even his own Liverpool fans don`t want him in the club anymore, despite his four year contract with the English club.

The reason why I'm mentioning this is to highlight a few important things. Firstly, professional soccer is not an easy game. In fact, it`s incredibly difficult on all levels.

It`s fiercely competitive and requires a lot of attention and hard work in order for anyone to succeed in it.

That means you must take it as a real mission and not just view it as some kind of an enjoyable way to make a lucrative living for a while where you get to treat yourself to a few of life's luxury spoils. It doesn't work like that.

Discipline, commitment, and a real genuine hunger to succeed are what separate the men from the boys in soccer. Always keep players like Mario Balotelli, Adrian Mutu, and even Maradona in mind.

Adrian Mutu became a cocaine addict who failed himself in both Chelsea and Fiorentina. Maradona turned out to be another drug addict who could have lasted longer in the game if he had more control over his life.

Take a good look at these guys and many others like them from over the years, and see what happens when you lose your focus on what really matters.

The players in these three examples (and there are many more) failed badly. They are the players who had it all – once - and then lost everything.

In some cases, they end up totally broke or forgotten by soccer fans, although Maradona is the exception here, rather than the rule. Most others become forgotten history or remembered for their decline rather than any success they might have had.

A couple of other past greats from the soccer archives, famous for their alcohol addiction, are Paul John Gascoigne, aka Gazza and George Best. Gazza is a former England midfielder who played for Newcastle, Tottenham, Lazio and Rangers during a distinguished career, yet today he is pretty much a broken man nowadays, hitting the newspaper headlines for all the wrong reasons.

We've also seen the rise and fall of that once great Northern Irish professional player George Best, who played as a winger for Manchester United and the Northern Ireland national team.

In his later years, George Best was an embarrassing drunk, primarily as a result of his undue love of alcohol and other forms of excess.

The list could go on and on, but the point is that soccer is a game where you need to take the job very seriously and work at maintaining mental focus and balance as much as you do developing your physical skills.

Once again, knowing the traps better enables you to prepare for them so that these things don't come up and grab you by your unawares, as they have done to so many others.

11. Not Using the Weather to Your Own Benefit

Bad weather is bad weather, you simply can't avoid it. Having said that, there are times when you can benefit from poor weather conditions. Now, you might be asking yourself how on earth you could benefit from bad weather because it's as bad for you as it is for every other player on the field.

Well, that's only true when you're unprepared. If, however, you played on the other team's weaknesses during different weather conditions, then you will become a force to be reckoned with.

OK, let's look at how to better prepare for playing in poor weather, namely windy, sunny, and rainy conditions.

Playing on Windy Days

One of the great benefits of playing on windy days is that you have a whole 45 minutes to play with the wind blowing against the other team. To take advantage of this you need to concentrate your tactics and playing style on long, high balls and crosses. This will cause problems for the keeper of the opposite team as well as his defensive line.

With strong wind against the goalkeeper, any attempts he makes to come out of his goal on crosses are reduced by 50 percent.

Additionally, the probability of his defensive players missing headers and crosses will increase since the direction of the ball changes by the effect of the wind.

In other words, it's quite unpredictable compared to still days, and that works in your favor.

Also on windy days, you`re encouraged to shoot from different distances. You do this for two reasons:

1. Slight changes in ball direction can easily deceive a goalkeeper and cause confusion for him. That means there's a higher probability of scoring goals for you.

2. Wind blowing towards the goal keeper will restrict his movement to some extent, making him heavier and less responsive than usual. In many cases, this one second delay is all that's needed to increase your chances of scoring past him.

Sunny Days - When the Keeper Can't See Properly

In general, a sunny day is by far the perfect day for playing soccer, especially when it's a cool sunny day.

However, there is one disadvantage for any goalkeeper who is playing with the sun against him, and that is the sunlight can prevent him from maintaining proper vision on the ball when it's high in the sky.

I have played as a keeper for a period of time, and believe me when I say that many problems occur when a keeper is unable to see an airborne ball coming at him.

To make sunny days work in your favor you have to play similar to how you would in the wind, and that is to rely on high balls when the sun shines directly on the goal area.

Your teammate's crosses as well as your headers will give the keeper a very hard time when the sun is in his face, no matter how good he is.

Rainy Days: Invest in Shooting and Rely on Rebounds

It's a fact, goalkeepers hate wet balls, and so they should for all the obvious reasons.

Rain undoubtedly affects players more so than goalies, especially with regards to pace and passing accuracy.

Even so, keepers have a tough time of rainy conditions too. Therefore, missed saves in wet conditions are to be expected and more tolerated under these circumstances.

When it's raining, goalkeepers find it particularly challenging to save shots and crosses simply because the ball is wet, and often muddy, and not necessarily because the shots were perfect.

In such conditions, a smart striker positions himself so as to take advantage of any rebound that might occur as the keeper fails to deflect or catch the ball.

12. You Don`t Have Enough Muscle

You won`t reach a high level of physical strength, agility and speed with a weak body. Moreover, you become the player who is most susceptible to tackles and injuries on the field during a game.

There are some players who are not physically solid nor do they have the muscle mass that I`m talking to you about, like Man City`s winger Jesús Navas, for example, but such players are not typical.

Case study one: Eduardo Da Silva

Eduardo Da Silva, commonly known as Eduardo or Dudu, is a Brazilian-born Croatian attacker who played for Arsenal between the years 2007 and 2010.

Da Silva was one of the most skilled strikers I have ever seen, but this is not just my opinion, many Arsenal fans thought so as well, and did his coach Arsene Wenger.

In fact, Wenger believed he was one of the best strikers to ever play in the English club and even said he could have made himself a true club legend - if only he was fit to play.

He was the type of striker you would love to see playing in your team`s shirt. He was fast, he was smart and he knew where to position himself, but best of all, Da Silva knew how to finish.

He possessed great skills for sure, and no one could deny him that. His only problem, and it was a big one for him, was that he wasn`t strong and solid.

In his first 27 games with Arsenal, Da Silva scored 19 goals for the team in addition to 12 assists before he got brutally injured. This happened in a league game against Birmingham City. City`s player, Martin Taylor, broke Da Silva's leg in one of the most shocking incidents in the history of the English premier league.

Da Silva had to spend at least nine months in the hospital because of his injury, and doctors tried hard to fix him up and prepare him for a full recovery.

Da Silva finally returned to the field in 2009. Sadly, he never managed to regain his edge or his position as the lead attacking player in the team. He left Arsenal after scoring just two goals in 11 post injury games.

Da Silva later spent four years in Ukraine playing for Shakhtar Donetsk, and he`s now playing in Club do Flamengo in Brazil, at the time of writing, despite being 32 years old.

The reason I'm telling you this is to illustrate through Da Silva`s story what can happen to all strikers (including you) if they don`t take care of their physical strength.

Da Silva was a high quality and very promising player. He could have become one of the best in the game, but it was his mistake (and Arsenal's) to not physically prepare for the demands of high intensity soccer.

He never spent the required time in the gym and therefore didn`t add enough muscle to support his legs against injuries.

Even when an accident is inevitable, having strong, well developed legs can lessen the damage caused by injury and also assist a faster recovery time. This is just one example of how a career can be lost in a nanosecond by the failure to prepare the body for the competitive game of soccer.

In Da Silva's case, his injury not only took one or two years from his career (and strikers` performance declines faster than defenders and goalkeepers), but it also made him afraid of using his full physical capacity to challenge defenders and attack the ball.

It became extremely easy for any defender to steal a ball from him or win a physical challenge, since other team's players soon got to know that he was afraid of reinjuring himself again and therefore would not put up much resistance when approached aggressively.

Case study two: Abu Diaby

The French soccer player Abu Diaby is adept in both attacking and defending. This man could have been one of the best defensive midfielders in the history of modern soccer if only he had been stronger.

The truth is he just couldn't handle the beating that comes with that sensitive position. He has suffered 28 injuries in different parts of his body, and played only two games in the last three seasons.

Diaby certainly short-changed himself. He really could have had a magnificent career if only he had supported his talent with enough physical strength to allow him to last longer at the top.

Case study three: Romelo Lukaku, Alexis Sanchez and Wayne Rooney.

Now it's time to look at the tough guys, the ones who did take control of their physical strength. Let's begin with the Belgian soccer star, Romelo Lukaku, nicknamed "The Tank" for his imposing strength and rock solid body. Lukaku, who plays as striker for Everton FC, is one of the best young talents in Europe at the time of writing.

He is the leading attacker for both his English club and the Belgium national team. Chelsea sold Lukaku to Everton in 2014 with a club transfer record of £28 Million.

The best thing about Lukaku is that he combines strength with speed, as well as having excellent finishing skills, all wrapped up in a single player.

I have watched him play for 30, maybe even 40 games now, and I have rarely seen him lose any physical challenge, even when pitted against famous center-backs like Chelsea's Jon Terry and England's former center-back Rio Ferdinand, both known as formidable players by their opponents.

Another two examples of players who cared about their physical strength are the attacking couple Alexis Sanchez (Arsenal) and Wayne Rooney (Man United).

They are two more prime examples of how combining speed, strength and elite finishing skills can make you truly excel on the soccer field and feared by your opponents.

Although Rooney might look solid by nature (he has been the same tough player since he was an 18 years old kid playing for Everton), the changes in Sanchez`s physique during the past six years is truly remarkable. It seems like he spends a fair amount of time at the gym, which is something I highly recommend for you too.

Aside from better protecting you from injury, having a strong, solid body also allows you to take on different roles on the field. However, to stay strong requires maintenance so there's no graduation from this, at least not while you're still competing in the game. You really can`t allow yourself to become a seasonal player if you hope to be one of soccer's greatest attackers.

A seasonal, physically weak player can only play against fast attacking teams or when his team is behind in the score and his coach is looking to throw all his attacking cards onto the field.

Worth noting is that seasonal players very rarely go on to become great attackers. Weak legs and weak muscles won`t help you once you get into higher competition.

Rules for Increasing Muscle

Rule #1: Spike up your protein intake.

The first thing you need to know is that running breaks down muscles. Most professional soccer players run from 8-10 kilometers on average to keep up with the game requirements.

To be able to maintain stamina you need proper nutrition, otherwise you could enter into a state of catabolism. Catabolism occurs when the body breaks down muscles to create the energy needed to supply the physical demands of the body.

To keep things simple, you have to include at least 1.5 grams of protein, per day, for each pound of your body weight. Once inside your system, protein helps to create amino acids, which are responsible for the muscle building process, hence being coined the "building blocks of life."

Amino acids also carry out many other important bodily functions, such as giving cells their structure, maintaining cartilage in joints, improve circulation and more besides.

Rule #2: Increase weights and decrease the range of your repetitions.

Your main goal, as a striker, when adding muscles to your body, is to increase your strength rather than your physical size. You must build muscles to support your body against fractures and injuries, but not too much.

Don`t forget that too much muscle (bulk) will slow you down and negatively affect your movements on the field.

In other words, you need to tone up and strike the right balance so that you have just the right amount of muscle, and not excessive muscle.

What this means is that you can't exercise like a bodybuilder. Bodybuilders want to get big, whereas you want to become lean and well-toned. Therefore, you will be using maximal strength exercises.

You perform these exercises by using simple, heavy weights, moved as fast as you can move them and with lots of rest between sets, like 2-3 minutes.

You will also only want to lift for a small number or repetitions for each set, something like 3-6 reps per set.

Remember, your goal here is to add more strength and ONLY enough muscle for you to maintain your performance.

Furthermore, each of these exercise sessions need to be kept short. Again, you're not supposed to be at the gym for half a day beefing up, just a short session where you focus on toning up.

Multi–joint exercises are the best for you. So instead of focusing on isolation exercises (each muscle group in one day, like leg-day, chest-day, shoulder-day, etc.), you work on multi–joint exercises. This means you`re incorporating more than just one set of muscles per exercise.

This will include exercises like squats, dead lifts, bench presses, clean and jerk, lunges and shoulder presses. These are the ones you should focus your attention on and incorporate into your training routine.

13. Not Knowing How to Deal with a Breakaway

In breakaways, you have two options. These will ensure your ball reaches the right place.

Option #1: Shoot in between the keepers legs. Anytime you don`t know where to shoot, and especially when the goalkeeper is so close to you that options are limited, then opt for a fast low ball in between his legs.

Unless the goalie is expecting you to shoot in between his legs, he won`t be able to catch your ball or deflect it away. The keeper's mind is often set on spreading and stretching his body to the outside, not to the inside. This is why you need to act fast and not make your decision look obvious.

Since humans are creatures of habit, your ball should reach the net in 50 percent of attempts. Your success rate should be even higher when you execute well-aimed shots. Remember, the ball is faster than the players on the field, and that includes the goalkeeper.

Option #2: Shoot while the keeper is leaving his goal. When you shoot with the keeper standing on his goal line (or near to it) he still has good chance to deflect your ball. His chance of saving your shot increases, as you get closer to him.

This is because your shooting angle becomes smaller and smaller the nearer you get. Therefore, the best chance of you getting the ball pass the keeper is to shoot while he is moving out, away from his goal line, but long before he gets close enough to restrict your options.

The more the goalie moves away from his goal line, the less chance he has of diving and stretching his body to save a ball heading for his goalmouth.

Another option available to you when you`re in a breakaway is when the goalkeeper is on the ground after attempting a save. Here you can dangle your foot over his shoulders, or elsewhere over his body, and then drop to the floor.

If all goes to plan, you get to take a penalty. I know this doesn`t sound moral for many people, but even so, when you`re team is losing you will find yourself doing anything and everything to score an equalizer or to win the game even.

If you don't play like this, there's a very good chance the other team will. It's just the way of modern soccer I'm afraid, so sometimes you just have to do what's necessary in the moment.

Referees do a remarkable job at making sure the teams adhere to the rules of soccer, and sometimes it seems as though they have eyes in the backs of their heads. Having said that, refs are still human, and that means they can't be looking at all things at all times.

In many cases, as you and the goalie are battling things out between yourselves, the ref will be far behind you. That means there's a chance he won't be in a good position to see the play.

So if you did your simulation or dive well, you should be able to get a penalty for yourself and your team.

You might even force the referee to send off the other team`s goalkeeper for his bad performance, or at least give him a yellow card.

Seriously, simulation, or feigning a move, can be your best option sometimes. The key here is not to overdo it. If you become infamous for faking plays by throwing yourself around a lot, news will soon spread and you will quickly gain a bad reputation.

This means referees will be on the lookout for you and watching you more carefully than they would do otherwise. So be careful, be cautious, and make any feints as convincing as possible at the time.

When a situation becomes desperate, it's always better to try something rather than to do nothing, but the secret is to hide your real intentions.

Let's look again at the brilliance of Inzaghi`s moves. He would often throw himself in the offside until he got a chance for a one-to-one.

When his plan succeeded he would get penalties and force the referee to show the other team's defenders or keeper colored cards. His tactics would also prevent the other team's players from going rough on him. In fact, this is one of the most used techniques by Barcelona players.

Since Barcelona has a different attacking style, one that requires them to pass the ball frequently between themselves, it makes them more susceptible to a barrage of challenges and tackles from the rival teams.

This style of play helps to win over the referee's protection and prevents the opponent's from to going too hard or too rough on them.

A lot of referees have zero tolerance when it comes to foul play, yet smart players can encourage others to attack them hard.

When this happens, they can either end up with a genuine foul or you can more easily make a feint around an aggressive move, thus producing the same result.

Players like Képler Ferreira, or Pepe (Real Madrid and Portugal), Martin Skrtel (Liverpool and Slovakia) or Luis Gustavo (Wolfsburg and Brazil), are easy to control when playing against them. You can take them out of the game with a single move, one word, or a convincing dive.

Alternatively, if you manage to get a rival player a yellow card early on in the game, say by exaggerating the effect of a tackle, you will then make your life a lot easier for the remainder of the game.

This is because the player will fear getting a second yellow card which would get him sent off the field.

More on Player Simulation

There is no question of doubt that faking a dive or "player simulation" as it's classified by FIFA (Fédération Internationale de Football Association) is a controversial issue.

The sole reason for performing fake dives is to deceive the referee into awarding an unjustified free kick or penalty. Is it right? No, of course it isn't. Is it widespread? Yes, it most definitely is. The problem is that just about everyone attempts it at some point, when the conditions are right of course.

Player simulation is especially common when things become desperate on the field for the losing side. This underhanded tactic has received a lot of bad publicity in recent years. This just goes to show how widespread it has become.

Whether it is something you will want to bring into your own style of play is a decision only you can make, based on own your ethics. Whatever your decision, it's important to note that others will continue to do it whether you do or not.

14. Not Frequently Pressuring the Referee

Pressuring the referee, even in the early stages of a soccer game, can work in your favor. Many times, and in many leagues, referees may favor one team over the other.

In cases like this it's important for the disadvantaged side to take the initiative and start to hassle the ref with every play. This is even more important for recorded games.

Just in case you're wondering, it is a fact that some referees love certain teams and it shows, no matter how much they try to hide their affection.

Michael Dean (the English referee) was once spotted celebrating a late goal by Manchester United; the man just couldn't contain himself.

Coaches know only too well what team a referee might like to see win, and so they let them know beforehand that they know about his preferences. This way the referee understands that he cannot show any signs of favoritism during the game.

If he does, he faces a full-on confrontation and possible embarrassment. This obviously puts pressure on him to be "fair" before the game has even gotten underway.

The Portuguese soccer manager, José Mourinho, gets in the face of referees a lot. In fact, he never misses any pre or post-game press conferences without playing mind-games with referees.

He does this to make sure his team doesn't get any undue hassles, things like cold or tough calls against his players. It's an effective strategy, and one which creates protection for the players in tough games.

Case Study: The Fergie Time.

The former Scottish manager for Manchester United, Sir Alex Ferguson, CBE, has had his moments during his time. He was well-known for the great effect he had on referees.

Research has shown that a referee would add an extra minute or two to the stoppage time just to avoid Ferguson's pressurizing and angry outbursts. This was infamously called "Fergie time." Here's a classic example of that "Fergie time."

In one game against Manchester City (an important competition and derby that can affect the league table for the rest of the season), the referee continued playing for a full six minutes after the official time.

This was despite the fact that the line man had announced only four extra minutes. Guess what? Manchester United went on to win that game by 4–3 in the stoppage time. This just goes to show how the referee`s decisions can be affected by small, calculated actions.

The Argentine manager, Diego Simeone, also known as Cholo, has a similar tactic when dealing with referees. His own Atlético Madrid players are also notorious for giving refs a hard time.

They implement various tactics during the game to pressure referees, especially when they feel they are getting a rough deal.

When playing against Barcelona or Real Madrid, the Argentinian manager and his players will gain so much leverage by pressuring the referee at two levels. The first is at the pre–game press conference and the second is on the field; once play is underway.

The players will question every single call the referee makes, as well as accuse him of helping the other "fancy" team to win the game by being unfair to them. Does it work? You bet it does.

Let's now look at how to perform this tactic to its best affect.

Pressuring the referee has to be a team effort if it's to be of any real use. In general, most refs are not that intimidated by a lone player. Therefore, it's better to gather your teammates around him and question his every call and every whistle.

Don`t make it easy on him to count fouls on you, instead become his worst nightmare, his constant pain in the side.

This is the last thing any ref wants. If you've done a good job, he will ease up on you and your side sooner or later. His job is tough enough as it is, so he doesn't want to add any additional, undue stress to is role.

Note that in many cases a referee will favor the home side over you, even though he's not always conscious of his favoritism, but it's there nonetheless.

Because of this he will sometimes give the home team free gifts at your expense. This is why you have to be tough on referees and refuse to accept their decisions as the final word.

15. Not Playing on the Referee`s Whistle

If you haven't heard the referee's whistle then always keep playing and never stop, not even if the ref's flapping his arms about frantically.

Don't even stop if other players around you have stopped. Just continue as if nothing has happened. Seriously, don't be influenced by anything or anyone, other than that whistle. There are two reasons for this

The first reason is because a referee will often question his own decision if he sees you're still moving with the ball. However, he is less likely to question his own decision if you have stopped playing.

This is because when you stop, you have pretty much conceded that you were in the offside trap, or accepted that the referee has perhaps just counted a foul on you for some reason. To stop means to concede.

The other reason why you shouldn`t stop until you hear the referee`s whistle is because you might just be having a false alarm. By that I mean you believe you have just landed yourself in the offside position, which may or may not be true.

However, don't hesitate if the whistle hasn't blown. If you do stop, you may be throwing away an otherwise easy chance to score a goal.

In addition to all this there will be situations where the defender responsible for setting the offside trap will stop suddenly. He does this assuming you`re in an offside position, or he may do it to even trick the referee into awarding his side with an indirect free kick.

Either way, just because he stops that doesn't mean you should. If the ref's whistle doesn't blow, your life has just gotten easier, and the defender has to restart his game, somewhat disorientated by his failure to pause the game. If you now find yourself in a one-to-one situation with the guy, he'll be easier to defeat because of his stalling.

My advice to you is to always keep running. You will lose nothing if you keep playing until the referee blows his whistle.

On the other hand, if you do stop and find that it was unnecessary, you will blame yourself for wasting a scoring opportunity. You might also get some flak from the other players and your coach, so take heed.

16. Failing to Master
What You`re Good At

Every player has something that makes him shine above all others, and this includes strikers. The roles may be the same, but the style of play and levels of achievement between individuals can vary a lot. Every attacker has some special skill, although it might not be obvious in his early days as a wannabe player.

Once discovered, he can then get to work at developing these newfound skills through commitment and hard work. This will put him on the right path for success, setting him apart from his peers.

We all excel, or could excel, at something, and this applies to anything in life. The problem is that many don't get the opportunity to find out what it is they're so good at. Because you're already a keen striker with some ability, the only thing remaining for you to do is to find out which areas you are best in.

You then need to zoom in and work at enhancing those areas still further. This could be your speed, your generosity (assisting style), your headers, or your physical strength.

Then again, maybe you have a knack at reading the game well and positioning yourself in the best place in preparation for the next move. Whatever it is you're good at, once you find it, you need to develop that skill until it/they become your signature move(s).

Just know this: no matter how great or how mediocre your style of play is right now, you will have at least one untapped skill that, once developed, will take you and your game up to a whole new level.

Generally speaking, most of my readers are not quite as old as I am, and so very few of you will be familiar with the name Jan Koller. Let me explain a bit about the man and the reason why I'm mentioning him here.

Koller was once on the Czech Republic`s dream team, alongside other greats like Pavel Nedved, Petr Čech, Tomáš Rosický and Karel Poborský.

Koller, who played for his national team between 1999 and 2006, was, and still is to this day, one of the biggest and tallest players to have ever competed in professional soccer.

He weighed in at 100 kilos and was 2.02 meters tall. This is not what you might call the ideal physique for playing competitive soccer, yet despite his lack of speed and agility, he was a great asset to his team.

He was useful because of his tall, strong physique, along with his superior heading ability.

In addition to his stunning headers (a guy standing at 2.02m doesn`t need to jump very high), and his very strong, accurate shots (both long and short range), he was one of the best players to play alongside.

This was because of his ability to assist his front line teammates by using his size, strength, and headers to best advantage.

He would play a similar role to that of the Egyptian striker Mido when he played at Tottenham, by assisting the fastest and the most skilled of his attacking teammates.

Despite his lack of speed, Koller became the all-time lead scorer for the Czech team, with 55 goals scored in just 91 games. This is a record that hasn`t been beaten since he retired in 2009.

The Story of a Great Defensive:

Midfielder Pep Guardiola

In a book about Bayern Munich`s manager, Pep Guardiola, entitled "Herr Pep," Guardiola talks about his role on the field and how he developed to become one of the best defensive midfielders in the world of professional soccer.

He achieved his ambitions despite lacking in speed and goal scoring skills. In fact, he didn't even have a very strong body.

When answering the question about how he made it, in spite of his drawbacks, Guardiola's answer was simple.

He said that he had realized early on that he would never be able to physically compete with many other players, so he knew he had to adapt if he were to excel in the game.

He decided to work on developing the skill of accurately reading the game and anticipating plays before they actually happen. This is something that he became very good at.

It made perfect sense to Guardiola, for him continue developing this ability still further. His new focus was to take his skill from being very good to exceptional. For Guardiola to get to the next level he studied countless hours of videos as he monitored other player's games and style.

He also took plenty of notes, and then he would test and then retest himself constantly. He never gave up and he never stopped trying to improve his game.

In fact, Guardiola worked relentlessly at improving himself for his entire life as a competing player.

This is a man who lasted for 11 years at Barcelona and then went on to become manager to one of the best teams in the history of soccer, Bayern Munich.

By realizing what he was good at, and then running with that skill until he became brilliant at it, was Guardiola's secret.

This should be your secret too. If you are to excel as a player and stand out from the pack, you have to zoom in on what you're good at and develop it until you become unbeatable.

This might be your speed, passing skills, dribbling, or shooting style. Whatever it is, you will know, or you will get to know when you start looking into your best points.

Believe me when I say, having superiority in a certain area, and developing one skill above all others, will help you to advance in your career.

And remember, it`s important to become the "number one" in that skill. People don`t care too much about second best, especially when it comes to choosing new players.

17. Running in a Breakaway

In any situation where there is only a single defender between you and the keeper, you may be forced to move over to the corner area where there is more space to play and make better decisions.

It's the same situation when you're in a one-to-one with the goalie and an opposition defender is closing in on you.

Once again you may be forced to move over to the corner area. However, being "forced" to make a move like this doesn't mean it is the ideal move to make.

Knowing Your Options

There are basically two other things you can do instead of heading toward the corner in situations like the ones above.

The first is to put your body in front of the keeper.

That means you won't have to go side-by-side with a defender; a position that allows him to perform a well-timed tackle that could result in you losing the ball. Instead, try your best to push yourself so that you're right in front of the goalie.

Doing this will give you a better shooting angle since it`s just you and the keeper, as well as a guaranteed penalty anytime the defender behind decides to tackle you or grab your shirt.

It`s a lot easier and much safer for a defender to perform a tackle sideways than it is to tackle a player who`s already in front of him. If he does try it on, then it`s a free penalty for you and an immediate red card for him.

The second option is to move toward an open angle rather than a dead one. Let me explain.

Instead of trying to escape by heading off toward the corner, or toward any side of the goal, all of which are dead angles anyway, try this: take your ball closer to the center of the penalty area.

This is where the goal is most open to you so it makes much better sense. It's also the place where you have a much higher chance to score compared to the side positions.

You're probably reading here thinking that it's not as easy as it sounds, and you'd be right, it's not easy, but then soccer's not any easy game.

These decisions also require speed and a lot of strength, and aggression. However, they are by far the best way to increase your chances of scoring a goal from a breakaway, or a counter attack.

18. Not Studying Your Opponent Properly

Not studying opponents is one of the biggest mistakes amateur strikers make. Ignoring the playing style of those who are marking you means you'll be on a hiding to nothing from the outset.

Note that I`m not referring to the broader game tactics here. What I`m talking about are the tiny details and pattern of mistakes that the rival team's defensive players and goalkeeper make.

Even great players have their weaknesses, and once identified, you can easily use these to your own advantage. However, if you don't know what they are then you lose and they win.

What Pre–game Videos Reveal?

Pre-game videos can reveal a lot, providing that is, you study them properly and ask an important set of questions as you view the footage. Such questions typically include:

- Speed: How fast are the defensive players? Who`s the fastest and who`s the slowest defender among them?
- Who`s the best defender in air plays, and who`s not good?
- Who`s not good at coverage?
- Who, if anyone, forgets to cover the offside trap?
- Who`s the agile player with the highest fitness levels, and who gets exhausted easily and can likely be beaten with speed?
- Who`s the most physically challenging and who's the least physically challenging?
- How good is the keeper in high balls, corners and crosses?
- How good is the keeper at long shots? How are his diving skills?
- How does the goalie deal with breakaways?
- Does the keeper spread himself out too quickly or does he like to wait?
- Does the goalkeeper cover for long balls? How tall is he? How can you use his height to your best advantage?

- Is there any pattern or flaw in the opposition's game plan overall that you can spot; little things that you can perhaps use to your advantage?

These are just some of the questions you can ask from the footage. Although you may not get answers to everything, your preparation for the game ahead will be so much better now compared to if you hadn't asked any questions.

Your own style of play and the style of your opponents will also help you to fine-tune your approach.

Depending on how you play will also determine what other questions you might want to ask in addition to the examples above.

What you're looking for here is an edge over the rival side. Being able to create and predict different game scenarios, based on what you know, will serve you much better than just turning up and hoping to win.

All Players Have Their Own

Frequently Repeated Patterns

Defenders have their own style of play, common patterns they repeat over and over despite how good or how bad they are.

Some players are more unpredictable than others, but when it comes to finishing, most will have a familiar pattern.

Case study: Gary Cahill, England and Chelsea`s center back.

Cahill is one of the best defenders in the English premier league (recently picked to be one of the 2015 premier league`s all-star team).

However, the man still has serious problems when it comes to setting offside traps and dealing with counter attacks.

In fact, anyone who's ever monitored Cahill playing style will tell you that his performance drops (sometimes quite dramatically) whenever he`s not playing next to Chelsea`s captain John Terry (one of the best European defenders of the last 10 years).

This is because Terry set rules and completes and cover`s his teammate`s mistakes.

Case study: Roberto Carlos

When Brazilian Roberto Carlos, a Real Madrid`s legend, finally retired from soccer, he confessed that his game suffered whenever the guy he was watching on the left flank went deeper inside the field and switched roles with another teammate.

During his last days at Spain, he and his team has got hammered and humiliated by the continuous motion and role switching done by Barcelona`s players.

Barcelona won because they watched. They studied the opponents and exploited their weak points. This is a habit you need to get into as well if you're to truly master your game.

Predicting defensive patterns and exploiting them is an incredibly powerful thing to have at your disposal, so make sure you take advantage of this.

19. Not Mastering Bicycle Kicks

Perhaps the most memorable goal any striker can have in his career is when he gets to score from a bicycle kick, also known as an overhead kick or scissors kick. Not only do the fans love it, but there is always plenty of applause and cheers from the crowds to show their respect.

These cheers will often come from both sides too, that's if it was a well-aimed and highly impressive shot. Such adulation makes you feel special, not least because the majority of soccer players suck at bicycle kicks.

This means the really impressive ones are few and far between, especially distant shots that land in the actual goal.

The 4 Rules to Consider When Performing a Bicycle Kick

Before you even think about a bicycle kick, you first need to get a sense of where the goal is in relation to where you are, as well as where the keeper is located at the time.

If you have ever watched Zlatan Ibrahimović's amazing 30 yard bicycle kick goal in the 2012 game with Sweden Vs. England, you will surely agree that this has to be one of the, if not THE, best bicycle kick ever recorded on TV. In fact, it was so impressive that it was chosen as FIFA`s goal of the year in 2013.

Ibrahimović was about 30 yards away from the goalmouth when he scored from this memorable shot.

He had an almost dead shooting angle for the ball, which was deflected by England`s keeper Joe Hart. Still, Ibrahimović turned this into a golden opportunity by scoring a wonderful goal nonetheless.

He did this because he managed to determine the positions of both the keeper - outside his penalty area - and the English side's goal before making his decision to go with the bicycle kick.

Remember, before performing a bicycle-kick, it`s necessary for you to consider where the goal and the goalkeeper are in relation to yourself. Failure to do this and you will likely fail.

You don't want get known as a "loose cannon" on the field, but that's what could happen if you waste or lose balls unnecessary. In short, make sure your decisions are calculated before deciding to act.

Know Your Distance

Your distance from the goal will determine which part of your foot you will perform the bicycle kick with. It's therefore important to get familiar with distances in relation to where you are at any given time.

When performing a bicycle kick, you get to use one of three parts of your outside foot, namely the middle, the toes or the far top of your toes. Which part of the foot you use depends on the distance from you to the goalmouth. Let's look at this in a little more detail.

Situation A: You are inside the penalty area, just a short distance from the goal. In this situation, the power of the kick is not your main concern.

What you need here is to make the shot sneaky enough so that it tricks the goalkeeper. Let's look at how to go about that. When you're this close to the goal, you have to strike the ball with the middle part of your outside foot.

You do this while contracting your body and keeping your knees bent, close to your chest. This way the ball hits the ground first, before bouncing into the goal. A successful bicycle kick like this, so close to the goal, will catch most keepers off guard.

If you have not yet learned how to perform a bicycle kick, this near goal approach is this one to start practicing with.

You will likely find things a bit awkward at the beginning, impossible even, but with enough practice it shouldn't be too long before you get to master it.

Situation B: You're on top of the penalty area and you want the ball to travel in a straight line toward the goal. In this situation, you concentrate all your power into your toes so that you can aim the ball in a straight line.

Your main aim is to direct the ball toward the upper part of the goal. This requires your chest is away from your knees a little. You will reach that stage when you see yourself falling on the upper part of your back instead of the middle.

Situation C: Here you are further away from the goal. This means you have to make sure the ball covers a greater distance when you kick it. This style of bicycle Kick will be from the "Ibrahimović's position."

In this case, you shouldn't wait for the ball to come close to your foot before you strike it. Instead, push your body a little toward the ball so that you catch it at a higher level from the ground.

The idea is to then kick the ball with your toes, not in a straight line but in a curve. This way the ball goes high before declining nearer the goal.

Striking the ball this way enables it to cover a larger distance without losing power. You will also get to trick the keeper providing your shot is well-aimed.

Not Worrying About Hurting Yourself

Your ability to learn the bicycle kick will depend to some extent on your toughness. In other words, you're okay getting a little hurt in the learning process.

There's just no way to master this move without plenty of practice and a few bumps and scrapes along the way. Just remember to use your hands when you`re landing so that you don`t fall hard on your back.

Mental Preparation Over and Over

Wayne Rooney once said that his visualization routine is what helps him to score great goals. This also includes goals scored from bicycle kicks of course. Rooney`s right too, visualization is a powerful technique and you would be wise to embrace it as well.

In this case you just imagine doing a bicycle kick over and over, with great power and accuracy.

There will come a point where you start to believe in yourself. Once this happens, you then get to turn your positive thoughts into positive actions on the field.

Visualization doesn't need much for it to become effective. I would suggest something like 20-30 minutes a day, and double that time the night before game day. This will improve your bicycle kicks like nothing else can.

Last Note: Don`t try to perform a bicycle kick when you have a better chance to score a goal from a header or with your foot.

This type of kick is usually a last resort option. The bicycle kick is not something you do for entertainment, not when you're competing to win a game.

Scoring goals for you and your team must always be the first priority, before showing off or playing with style.

20. Not Putting Enough Work into Improving Your Shot Accuracy

When asked what the most important basic skill is to learn, I always suggest the passing skill. As a soccer striker, you need to be able to send that ball to exactly where you need it to end up.

I want you to compare any professional striker with someone who plays striker in your local team. If you don't have a local team, just pick someone from another average team or league that you "know of."

You will soon get to see how inferior the shots are from the average player when compared to the pro.

113

Top strikers know where the goal is at any given time, and they also know how and where they should send their balls.

Having some kind of close relationship with the ball is not unique to soccer players either. You can see a similar thing in all ball games like handball, basketball and even table tennis.

Search on YouTube for David Beckham and Roger Federer. You will find some great footage of these guys working miracles with their shots. Videos like these are great for getting a little inspiration.

You must practice at enhancing your shots all the time. Never think you are as good as you're going to get because there is always room for still more improvement.

You Have to Be Able to Shoot from Anywhere on the Field

You need to practice sending your balls from every single position on the soccer field. After all, you have to create quick solutions for both yourself and your team whenever needed.

Start practicing by picking some awkward places on the field. This might include shooting from the toughest angles and the widest positions. Keep practicing from these positions over and over until you become great at it.

Low balls, high balls, bicycle kicks, free kicks and so on; make sure you cover the lot. Don`t leave a single place where you can score a goal from without practicing from that spot.

Techniques Are Mastered with Practice

No matter what advice you get on how to shoot a ball, or increase your accuracy, none of it counts until you act. In other words, you won`t see any improvement in your shooting style until you practice. You will only get to learn the right techniques once you`ve done things the wrong way.

Remember, mistakes, failures, call them what you will, are a necessary part of learning. Shooting accuracy is proportional to the number of shots you practice. In other words, the more you practice, the better you'll become. It really is as simple as that.

The 500 x 30 Routine

Practice by shooting 500-1000 shots at the goal every day. Remember to do this from different angles and from different places around the field.
Continue like this for 30 consecutive days without breaking. Providing you don't skip practice, your performance will improve a lot in just a single month.

21. Letting an Opponent Destroy Your Focus

Some defenders will try to destroy your focus and mess with both your physical and mental game. The only way to prevent their efforts is by keeping your mind focused on the game, your game.

If you let these defenders get to you, they will eat you alive. Some defenders are slow and that can make them aggressive when they're on a losing run.

Others are unable to keep up with the game in general and feel that the only way to slow you down is by messing with you.

Great defenders will never use immature tactics against their opponents. Still, not all defenders are great, and you need to be aware of this.

Case Study 1: When Zidane got angry.

A sad day for soccer players and fans alike was in the 2006 World Cup where Italy Vs. France. The Italians were perhaps the only ones to relish in the moment, but for everyone else it was sad event.

What happened was that the French midfielder, Zinedine Yazid Zidane (nicknamed Zizou), got sent off by the referee.

His offence was that he head-butted the Italian defender, Marco Materazzi, in the chest, 19 minutes into the extra time.

It was a hard blow that sent the Italian to the ground. The commentator at the time said: "Why oh why would he do that in his final international?"

When asked about the incident later, Materazzi confessed to provoking Zidane. He said that he insulted both his mother and his sister in an attempt to get under the player's skin. It worked too.

If only Zidane could have restrained himself a while longer. Perhaps then, his team might have won their second World Cup.

This was the worst possible farewell ever for a soccer legend like this. Zidane remains an icon in the eyes of the French public, but this one incident will haunt him forever.

Case Study 2: Cavani Vs. Jara

In June 2015, I was watching the quarterfinal game in Copa America between Uruguay and Chile. Late in the game, the referee sent off the Uruguay striker, Edinson Cavani, but not for the usual foul play. This was the most bizarre sending-off I have ever seen. Here's what happened.

In the 63rd minute of the game, the Chile defender, Gonzalo Jara, did a crazy thing. He poked his finger, or appeared to poke his finger, up the Uruguay striker's backside, but this was not the end of the incident.

Things got worse when Jara then threw himself on the floor and claimed that Cavani had hit him in the face.

Cavani was in a state of fury after the referee showed him his second yellow card of the game. Uruguay lost their most valuable player and their only attacking option on the field. They then went on to lose the game 1–0 to Chile.

Later on, Chile`s defender, Jara, did not go on to play in the championship after receiving a three-game ban. Even so, he still managed to get what he wanted by stopping Cavani`s danger with a cheap trick in that all-important game.

How to Avoid Dirty Tactics

The first thing you need to avoid dirty tactics, like the one above, is a level head. It's all too easy to lose control in a moment, especially when the heat is on. You have to rise above the one who's playing unfair, and be careful not to stoop to their level.

Note that players like Jara are not mentally stable, how could they be by such actions?

What they definitely are is bugging and irritating, but then only if you allow them to get under your skin. Understand that if you respond in a negative way to their bizarre actions then they win, and you lose.

Whenever any player bugs you, the best thing to do is channel all your energy into the game, not the incident.

Case Study 3: Sweet revenge: Ruud Van Nistelrooy

YouTube the term "Ruud Van Nistelrooy best celebration ever." You should find a Video of Nistelrooy acting a bit silly.

This incident came about as a result of a wasted penalty for the Dutch striker. It happened when an opposition defender from the Andorra side approached Van Nistelrooy and started laughing at him.

Van Nistelrooy kept a cool head and did not take the bait, at least not notably. He did fail to score though. What he did to get revenge was to wait until he scored his next goal.

He then sprang into action by running over to the Andorran defender as he celebrated his goal. He then waved his arms up in the air in an almost childlike fashion, right in front of the opponent's face.

Was this the perfect revenge? Well it wasn't bad but it wasn't perfect either. Look at is as a compromise.

There were no red cards given, but he did receive a yellow card for unsportsmanlike behavior.

22. Not Practicing Visualization

The visualization technique is one of the greatest mental exercises around. In fact, many athletes and soccer players around the world swear by it.

Those who practice visualization will be able to achieve more goals than those who do not. There are three great reasons to get into visualization:

- **One**: It will help you predict new scenarios and better prepare you for any game.

- **Two**: Visualization enhances your skills. This works by you visualizing your decision-making process and performance. You keep doing this over and over until you believe what you see. There comes a point where you are able to put those visualizations into actual practice on the field. The consequence of this is that you get to make faster and more accurate decisions during the game.
- **Three**: Visualization won't exhaust you. You can perform it anytime, anyplace, anywhere.

In an interview, Manchester United's Wayne Rooney talked about his pre–game rituals. He attributed a great part of his success to his daily visualization routine. Rooney is not the only soccer star to sweat by its benefits either.

Rooney would spend the whole night before the game visualizing events on the field. He would be playing in the exact kit he'd be wearing on the day, and performing well against the opposition. He would score some great goals for his side and make some impressive moves.

Rooney said that the reason behind this visualization was simple. It was so that he could mentally prepare for every single situation he may face during the actual game. He said it acted as his "game memory." His "game memory" as he called it, were his last visualizations embedded into his mind.

Rooney said that visualization helped him to score some of the most amazing goals early on in his career. It helped him to hit far posts from 30 yards, and sometimes more.

He also got to perform Messi type tricks like dribbling through many opponents in a single play. None of this, he thinks, would have been possible without visualization.

All these things came about because he had imagined them to be true and so they became his reality. He attributed his success as a youngster to both hard work and visualization. The more he visualized, the better the results.

Importance of Clarity

Most people who manage to create success for themselves use visualization. In fact, many will use it as an integral part of their daily routine. The reason for this is simple; achieving goals requires clarity, and visualization helps to clarify the mind.

Successful people will often say accomplishment is like a journey, and they're right, it is. The reason why so many people fail in life is not because they lack mental ability or physical talent.

It's because they lose their way. At some point they stray from the path and don't even realize it. Visualization techniques help you focus on what matters most and remain focused.

Distraction is a killer. It kills more dreams and ambitions than anything else. Distraction upsets the flow of things; it takes you away from your primary goal.

Distraction also stops momentum and dwindles enthusiasm. Twenty-first century lifestyles are full of unwanted distractions.

Many don't realize just how much their mind jumps from one thing to another in the course of five minutes.

If you could see written down on paper what your mind processes in just a few minutes, you wouldn't believe your eyes.

This is why it's important for ambitious soccer players to learn how to focus and stay on track. When you're working hard on your game, it is all you should be working on. Visualization is a great tool to use and there are no drawbacks to it at all.

As you read here, visualization might come across to you as little more than fantasizing. All I can say to that is don't knock until you try it. I can assure you that this is a tried and tested method.

All kinds of people from all walks of life use visualization all the time, and to great effect. This includes athletes, actors, singers and musicians, to name just a few.

Start using your imagination to create what you desire in life and great things will surely come to pass, of this I am certain.

23. Not Increasing Your Shooting Rate

A positive side to aggression is that you shoot a lot at the goal, from all sides, at all angles, and from all positions. Rival players and their goalkeepers fear formidable strikers. The best strikers are tough and aggressive, but in a channeled way, not in an underhanded way.

The important rule is to never wait for certainties. By that I mean don't only shoot when there's a golden opportunity to score.

Whenever you get a shot at the goal, no matter how slim, go for it if there are no better options.

The Difference between
Selfishness and Trying Harder

You won't always get a shot at the goal just because you have the ball in your possession. There will be cases where you're at a dead angle, or there is simply no clear shot available.

In situations like these, it's wise to pass the ball on to a better positioned teammate. Strikers who shoot at the goal regardless of whether there's a potential to score or not are playing a selfish game. This is unacceptable behavior in a team sport like soccer.

The main aim for strikers, and all team players come to that, is to play for the benefit of the team as a whole.

Everyone likes a little personal glory, but this should never come at the cost of the team. Selfish behavior and showing off will be the downfall of any player, no matter how talented he may be.

Case Study:The Shooter: CR7

Watch any game for Real Madrid or the Portuguese national team and you will see a familiar pattern. Cristiano Ronaldo comes out on top of the "who threatens the goal most" list for both teams.

Ronaldo scored 61 goals in 2014, with his shot accuracy at 54%. His conversion rate was just above 30%.

In fact, his conversion rate was just 12% at the beginning of the season. This tells us that Ronaldo has had at least 3-4 shots per game, which is pretty impressive by all accounts.

Remember what I told you about aiming high and setting goals that are 10+ times bigger than usual? Well, this is the same thing.

The more you put into something, the more you will get out of it. This doesn't mean shooting at the goal when there are better options available.

It just means be bold, and go for every "opportunity" that presents itself, even when it's a tough call. You need to make this a habit so that it becomes part of your playing style, of who you are.

24. Surrendering to Booing

Some strikers are too fragile by far. These are the guys who are affected by the cursing and booing from the other team's supporters. Okay, so it's not a pleasant experience, especially if it lasts for the entire 90 minutes of a game, as it can do at times.

Even so, the more you let it get to you, the worse your performance will become. This is bad news for you but great news for the opposing fans because their tactics have worked.

It's crucial that you learn how to grow a thick skin. Just know that thin-skinned strikers will never last for long. You need to learn how to respond, or not respond, as the case may be.

This is the only way to overcome jeering from the opposing fans. Seasoned players know how to manage such crowds, and how to give an appropriate reply when needed.

Racism – The Portuguese and the African Trio - Case Study

When the two African players, Samuel Eto'o and Yaya Touré played for Barcelona, they had it rough. These poor guys would receive constant racial comments from the crowds.

Perhaps the worst of it all was when they had to listen to opposition fans making monkey sounds. Sometimes, they would even throw bananas at them, especially Samuel Eto'o.

How do you think you would survive under such hostile situations as this? It takes a real man to turn a blind eye to such racist taunts, that's for sure, but this is exactly what those guys did.

They would play at their best and perform with impressive skill, refusing to take the heckler's bait. The result was always one up in favor of Samuel Eto'o and Yaya Touré.

Do you think these taunts affected them in the privacy of their own heads? I think the answer to that has to be an emphatic yes, of course they must have been.

But you see, it is how you deal with situations like this which determines the outcome.

I would go as far to say that the best performance from the Africans was when they actually received these racial insults. You might be wondering how this can be so, but the answer is quite simple.

These are players with lots of talent and plenty of drive, and so they turned their anger into positive energy.

They had a game to play and were all fired up beyond belief, so they played like their life and reputation depended on it.

Ronaldo is good at this too. Since he is one of the best players in the world, he's also the most threatening player on his team. Because of this, most of the rival team's fans like to give him what you might call "a special treatment."

They do this as a way to get under his skin and throw him off, but it never works.

Watch videos of Real Madrid games and you will see what I'm talking about. A lot of the time Ronaldo receives a fair amount of cursing, shouting and booing from the rival fans.

How does this soccer sensation respond to it all? He does what he knows best and keeps scoring goals.

He shows no sign of irritation or distraction at all. This is usually enough to shut even the most hardened of hecklers up.

All great players keep cool under pressure. If you are easily upset then you need to work at growing that thicker skin.

Learn how to channel your energy into your game, and not into your inner self. Learn this and you will fare much better when confronted by hostile crowds.

Here are a few examples of other players who tend to thrive when under pressure from jeering crowds.

Robin van Persie and Samir Nasri, when they playing against Arsenal. Luís Figo and Ronaldo (the Brazilian) when playing against Barcelona. Luis Suarez, when playing against Chelsea, Man United and Juventus. Frank Lampard when playing against West Ham United.

The list could go on.

Some high-profile players crack under pressure and fail to perform well when jeered at. Iker Casillas is one of them.

Casillas' performance has declined during the last few years. He gets angry a lot and loses his focus because of it.

He makes plenty of blunders whenever he listens to Real Madrid fans at the Santiago Bernabéu calling for him to retire or leave the team. In other words, Casillas takes the bait and the hecklers love it.

The result: Hecklers 1 Casillas 0.

Of course, no one wants to put up with heckling, but it can be part of the game like it or not. It is the responsibility of the player to toughen up in these situations.

When all's said and done, you will never be able to control the verbal chanting of a rowdy crowd. Let's not forget too, some of these players get paid big bucks.

A top striker can't expect eight million plus dollars a year for nothing. Becoming all sensitive to jeering and criticism is not good for the player and it's not good for his club. He might not like what he hears sometime, but letting it affect his game is not part of the deal.

The best response to any form of jeering is to prove your worth on the field. The opposite of that is to not prove your worth on the field and let your performance decline by your sensitivity.

If you lose focus, or you get angry, or show frustration, you have lost and they have won. Seeing you crack is just what hecklers want to see for their efforts. Whether they win or lose is largely down to you and your reaction to the situation.

I hope you can now see the importance of remaining cool and staying in control. Ignoring abusive crowds won't make them go away from the grandstands. What it will do though is remove them from your head, which will allow you to get on with your game.

By the way, when you don't take the bait, it is the hecklers who start to get agitated and upset. In other words, their unpleasant jeers backfire on them.

You have nothing to lose and everything to gain by growing that thick skin.

25. Not Daring to Dribble

Only the best of the best strikers will dare to dribble through an entire defense line. It's not a feat for the faint hearted, that's for sure. You need courage, tenacity, and bags of confidence. When a striker takes on such a task he believes with all his heart that he can do it.

Case Study: The Argentinian magicians.

Have you ever seen Messi`s wonderful goal against Getafe? This has to be one of the best solo goals of all time.

It`s not just great, it's exceptional. Messi took the ball before the center line and went through five Getafe players. He then went on to beat their goalkeeper before planting the ball into an empty net.

Also check out the Brazilian, Diego Maradona, and his goal against England in the 1986 FIFA World Cup. Here you will see what real courage the man has. It`s like the Messi`s goal that I mentioned.

Here Diego dribbles from behind the center line. He goes through four English players and their keeper before scoring a wonderful goal.

This style of play requires not only speed but also a lot of skill. On top of that there must also be aggression, a lack of fear, and some understanding of the opponents.

These combined attributes are what makes this man a true soccer icon. Maradona is an all-time great according to his fans, even to this day. This is despite his past heroin addiction and other controversial behaviors he became infamous for.

The Brazilian soccer star, Ronaldo de Assis Moreira (more commonly known as just Ronaldinho), is perhaps the best of the best players to ever touch a ball when it comes to his pure dribbling genius.

He might not be the best all-round attacking midfielder or forward of all time, but he is certainly up there with the greats when it comes to dribbling and other ball skills.

Watch any of his video clips against Real Madrid and you will marvel at his talent. Ronaldinho managed to make a team of high-profile players from the most expensive team on earth look like a bunch of amateurs, and he did this single-handedly.

The secret to his success is no secret at all. Ronaldinho has professional skill, he possesses great ball control, and he is brave beyond belief. He worked relentlessly at becoming who he is today and went on to achieve greatness as a result.

You too can become an excellent dribbler. At least if you have the base skills required you can, along with patience, persistence, and a real hunger to develop as a leading player.

Consider dribbling as if it's some sort of a "man thing," not dissimilar to approaching a woman and asking for that first date (bear with me a while and you will see how the same attributes apply to both).

Just like a good relationship, dribbling is something that has needs nurturing if it's to work in your favor. The thing that usually holds players back in this area is a lack in self-belief. Just like a first date, dribbling takes that first step to prove to yourself you can do it.

To be good, you have to be fearless not hesitant. You also need to have plenty of confidence, not timidity. Most importantly, don't let any failed attempts to succeed knock you back.

Once you pass the early obstacles, you can only get better over time. Furthermore, once you've got the fundamentals of dribbling pinned down, you will see your own unique style begin to develop.

Technique won't be your biggest hurdle though, courage will. You can only build courage from practical experience, and not through a textbook, tape, or other media. Sure, you can learn from other media, but at the end of the day it is action that builds bravery.

Once you have both your own unique style pinned down, and oodles of courage to boot, then your opponents had better watch out!

26. Not Learning from Videos and Duplicating

With so much access to online video archives, I'm amazed that so many young soccer players fail to use this invaluable medium.

This is something which can really help to enhance your game. My advice to you is to study great players on video and watch them a lot.

The best thing about audio-visual is that you can view it from beginning to end, you can pause, rewind, fast-forward, and even continue to watch it over and over again if you need to.

This way you get to pick up on every little thing that's of any use to you.

I would even go as far to say that studying other players on video should become an obsession. Note I say "study" and not watch. There is a big difference here. We usually watch soccer for pleasure, and that means the mind is in a different place than when we study.

When we study something, we are looking at it in a completely different light. We have an attention for detail that just isn't there when we watch a game for pleasure purposes only.

Learning from the soccer greats is what I call a healthy obsession. It is where moderation has no place for the most ambitious among us. This is especially true when you're young and eager to speed up your development as fast as you can.

Between YouTube, Vimeo, Dailymotion, Veoh, and Metacafe, there shouldn't be anything you can't find from the world's soccer archives. Best of all is that there is plenty of software out there these days that let you download your favorite vids to your computer.

The Ugly Truth - You`re Running out of Time

The hard truth is that the life of a top soccer striker is short lived, at least from a career perspective. Therefore, the sooner you start to develop and grow your skills the better. The modern world moves at a fast pace anyway, but this is especially true for active soccer players.

By the time you reach your early to mid-twenties, most of your skills and attributes should be at 60% to 70% of their full potential. In other words, you are almost at your best with only a few tweaks and modifications required to maintain and develop what you already have.

The older you are, the more you are racing against time to make a splash in the world of soccer. This is especially true for life as a top striker. These aren't ageist remarks; they are simple facts for logical reasons.

Soccer, along with other sports, can seek to take on people within a certain, youthful age bracket for obvious reasons. This is not the case for most other professions where ageism is against the law.

Don't Waste Time Planning and Creating Schedules

I have always found "doing" a better option than "thinking," and especially over-thinking. In a fast moving world like soccer, it is actions more so than thoughts that get you noticed.

Of course, you have to make plans before you can act on them. Even so, it's the micro-management you have to avoid; the majoring in minor things.

The fastest way to learn anything new is to get to work on it as soon as possible, and without wasting precious time. I wouldn't even bother about preparation too much, other than to make sure you're safe before continuing.

Fast, decisive action allows you to do more and master something quicker. There's too much time wasted on thinking about the best way to do a thing, or looking too deep into the ways to approach it.

You must have heard the saying: "Go in at the deep end and you will soon learn to swim?" What it means is know the basics of what's required and then just get stuck in without further ado.

You can usually see what kind of approach you take by looking at your life in general. For example, ask yourself how you manage your life now?

Do you produce fast results by your actions, or do you spend more time thinking about a thing than you do acting on it.

If yes to the latter, then at least try the opposite approach and start to think less and do more. Try it for just a month to see the difference. The chances are you will like it better. Action gets you more pumped up than thoughts.

It creates momentum and produces faster results. Many of us don't realize just how paralyzed we have become by "justifiable" procrastination. Once you can break the habit, you're going to make a positive shift to your mindset.

You will become more productive than you've ever known. When you transform from a thinker to a doer, you will on the right path to becoming a high achiever.

Using Cameras

Recording your performance using video can be an invaluable tool. Footage like this can reveal so much more about the way you play. This includes highlighting things that would have otherwise gone unnoticed.

You can use video to identify your strengths and point out any weaknesses you might have. It is only when you get to identify flaws in your game that you can set to work on fixing them. Video can help with this.

Thinking about stuff after an event, and having things explained by others is all fine and dandy. Even so, the more tools you have at your disposal the better you will fare.

It is only when you can see yourself in pictures (moving and still shots) that you get to appreciate the power of the lens.

Your aim is to find out all there is to know about yourself and the way you perform on the field. If you want to see your playing style for what it is, and expose any weak areas you might have, then use cameras, and use them a lot. You won't regret it.

Today we have a real advantage over the players of yesteryear. This is because most of us have Smartphones, Tablets or Phablets at our disposal. All these devices have inbuilt video functions, which makes recording both cheap and easy.

The most important thing for you to acknowledge is that even if you're a good player right now, exceptional even, you still have more to give.

No player should ever concede to the notion that he's about as good as he's likely to get. This just isn't true. There is always room for more.

Give me recorded footage of any amateur player and I can tell you all kinds of things about the individual. It won't take me long to spot the good and not so good areas of his playing style.

More than 95 percent of the time I'm right in my assessments. This is not because I have any kind of magic skill for this. It's simply because I have learned how to "observe" a player's performance as opposed to "watching" it.

All you need to know is that something can show up on film that is not always obvious by other methods of observation.

From video you get to identify bad footwork, distractions, any lapse in reading the game, and so on. It all comes out on film, once you know what to look out for.

I recommend you ask a friend, or anyone who has good knowledge of soccer, to record you performance. It's also better if they know how to use a camera to best effect.

The first few attempts to record you in action might be a bit hit-and-miss, but that's okay. Just keep at it and you will soon have some great footage taken from the best shooting angles.

You see, no matter what great advice and tips your coach gives you, there is nothing quite as valuable as seeing yourself play.

If you want to fix, fine-tune, and add new skills to your toolkit, then you need to start recording your performances.

27. Not Using Both Legs Equally

Having the ability to use both legs equally is fundamental for any good striker. It is the second most important skill behind being aggressive and tenacious on the field.

Look at the most successful strikers in soccer today and you will see that they can all play with both feet to great effect. Some of the most famous names are:

- Cristiano Ronaldo
- Messi, Rooney
- Edinson Cavani
- Luis Suarez
- Radamel Falcao
- Karim Benzema

- Neymar da Silva Santos Júnior
- Sergio Agüero
- Diego Costa
- Didier Drogba
- Zlatan Ibrahimović
- Robin Van Persie
- Edin Džeko
- Carlos Tevez
- Robert Lewandowski
- Thomas Müller

All these players are capable of using both left and right foot equally, and from any position.

I know that you can still be good, or even great, with one leg, but you won't be exceptional.

This is because you don't have the luxury of choosing where and how to receive the ball inside the penalty area.

In most cases, when you find the ball in front of you, all you can do is deal with it as best you can, with your only workable foot.

How to Train a Weak Foot

To train a weak foot you need to start slow. It can be an awkward feeling at first, so you have to ease things in until the weak foot gets used to the ball. The best approach is to begin with easy drills.

This will include things like simple passing drills, and kicking a ball against a wall and then receiving it with the same weak foot.

You can also work at flipping the ball, and then doing a back heel kick. As you practice these drills, make sure to use both the inside and the outside of your weaker foot. Once you start to get comfortable playing the ball with your weaker foot it is time to work on accuracy.

Focusing on Accuracy

Begin by using some foul sticks and placing them in different locations on the field. Your aim is to kick the ball at them from different angles and positions. Here you are focusing on enhancing the accuracy or sensitivity of your leg.

It doesn't matter if your balls come out weak or inferior compared to those you send with your dominant foot. In fact, it's expected. Remember, patience and persistence is what prevails in the end.

Working on Power

By this stage you should be more comfortable using your weaker foot. You should also have some degree of accuracy. Now it's time to look at strengthening both the weaker foot and its leg.

Begin by taking different positions outside the penalty area, both near and far. The idea here is to work on sending fast, strong balls towards the upper and lower corners of the goal.

You will find this to be the toughest part of all. Even if your accuracy is quite developed by now, it will be of no use to you unless you can pack a strong kick.

Again, don't give up or lose hope. Even if it feels like an impossible task, I can guarantee that you will get better at it the more you practice. It might not feel like that right now, but you will get there, winners always do.

This stage may take you a month of continuous practice before it starts to feel more natural. Once you get better at it, you can then work on playing backwards and even practice bicycle-kicks if you feel confident enough.

Remember to never give up just because it's tough. The more obstacles you can get over as you develop your game, the better you will become.

28. Playing Between Two Center Defenders

Playing between the center backs, as opposed to in front of them, gives you a definite edge. It benefits you with crosses and through-passes (especially in crosses).

The reason for this is because you're positioning yourself behind one of the center backs.

When you do this, he can't keep his eyes on you and maintain a perfect position to catch a header.

This position is:

-   Right in front of the goal. This gives you a wider angle to shoot from and allows you to easily place the ball anywhere with less dead angles to contend with.

- Right in front of the other center back. Here you get to reach the crossed ball at a suitable height before it reaches him.

Another smart move you should consider is to stand behind the other team's defense line, in the offside.

You do this when they are all busy monitoring the ball at the center line.

Your position gives you a better overall view of the ball. It will also prevent the opponents from marking you or monitoring your movements, which obviously makes it easier for you to surprise them when the time is right.

The way to achieve this position without detection is quite easy. All you need to do is to run a few meters to the back, get in the onside, and then move into the empty space.

Defenders are not robots, nor do they have rear view mirrors to see who's behind them. So you need to stand at their blind side and benefit from their mistakes.

29. Not Considering Your Role as Your Team`s First Defensive Player

In the event of failed attacks, or whenever the goalkeeper catches a corner or a cross, you need to spring into action.

The first thing you have to do is delay the counter attack for as long as possible. You do this by preventing the keeper or the defender from passing the ball on, using whatever method you can.

The moment your opponents get the ball back into play is the moment you have a dangerous counter attack going on. This is not what you want to happen before your teammates get to take their positions.

So how can you delay the action? Well, to begin with you can stand in front of the keeper and obstruct his moves. You might even have an opportunity to steal the ball from him. You can also create fouls if that's the better alternative.

The point is that you need to be both creative and quick to be effective. The more you hold things up, the better chance your team has to rearrange themselves and prepare for any counter attack.

Two Defensive Roles for Smart Strikers to Consider

It is always a good idea to work on pressuring the goalkeeper whenever he has the ball in his possession.

The keeper is the first player to start an attack in most corner kicks and crosses. Your job, as a striker, is to delay him until your defenders are back in their own half. When done well, the chance for the rival side to create a counter attack diminishes by a lot.

Some goalkeepers are excellent at sending long balls and creating counter attacks for their teams. This is why you should always study the style, the abilities, and any flaws of rival players before a game. Preparation is the key to success.

The former Argentine goalkeeper, Roberto Abbondanzieri, was great at creating scoring opportunities for his team. Just give him the ball and watch how far and how accurate he sends it to his attacking teammates.

His ability was quite amazing. You need strong focus when playing against keepers of this type. This is because you never quite know where they might send the ball to.

One of your roles as your team's attacker (and sometimes the only attacker), is to put pressure on the opposite team's defenders.

Your aim is to keep them in their own side of the field and prevent them from advancing to outnumber your team in the middle.

As a striker, you will always be close to the middle or the center of the field when your team under attack. Some strikers, however, forget themselves and start going after the ball even when it's in the third side of the field.

This is a dangerous move, not least because it leaves the centerline without anyone there to protect it.

The consequences of this are as follows:

- It allows an extra opponent to help generate an attack on your side.
- You are no longer there so you don't have the opportunity to create fast counter attacks whenever a teammate steals the ball and decides to send it to your team's front line.

Sometimes the other team might have a highly skilled center back in their squad. Players like these need special attention from you.

The best thing you can do with players like this is to put pressure on them using whatever means are at your disposal. Your job here is to stop them from advancing with the ball to your midfield or penalty area.

A talented center back can be good at passing or shooting, or even both. All you need to know is that if they're exceptional, they need more attention than if they were average to good.

Defenders, like the Brazilian David Luis, Belgian Thomas Vermaelen, and Danish Daniel Agger, are some of the most skilled center backs in modern soccer.

All three of these guys are renowned for their excellent attacking skills, their good footwork, and their strong, accurate long-shots.

Agger himself has scored 12 international goals for his team, Denmark, in only 67 Caps. To put this in some perspective, it is a number close to the scoring ratio of some of the most skilled midfielders in European soccer.

30. Not Having Proper Communication with Your Fellow Strikers

If you want to understand how good communication works, then look no further than FC Barcelona. This is a team that managed to win the trilogy, which includes the Spanish League, the Spanish Cup and the UEFA Champions League.

They did it because they play well as a unit, and that means they communicate effectively. So what makes them so complete?

Well, it is their total understanding of each other, their selflessness, their deep desire to win, and a strong team spirit. The magical trio on the front line, namely Neymar, Luis Suarez and Messi, are the envy of every team the world over.

Watch any of their games and you will see that every one of them is scoring goals and every one of them is assisting.

Even during the last few games of the season, where Messi was competing against Ronaldo for the league top scorer, you would find Messi (the number one penalty taker in Barcelona) leaving his penalties for Neymar to take. He did this as a way of repaying him for his magnificent assists.

The other side of good communication is the lack of interaction between players. We can use the French team, Paris Saint-Germain FC, to illustrate.

Despite having won both the French League and the French Luck, this is a team that could be so much better than they are.

Their main problem is the sad lack of understanding between their two attacking players. I'm talking about the Swede Zlatan Ibrahimović, and the Uruguayan Edinson Cavani. These guys are not on the same page most of the time.

Here's the likely cause of this problem:

Both Ibrahimović and Cavani wanted to take the center forward role. Likewise, both of them hate playing on the wings.

This was such an issue that Cavani asked to be sold on at the next transfer market if the coach insisted he played as a winger rather than a center forward.

Anybody supporting the team can easily spot the tension between these two attacking sensations.

Case study: The rise of Lionel Messi

Although he's a wonderful player, and one of the best to ever touch the ball, Messi didn't always shine. It was only when Pep Guardiola (his former coach at Barcelona) decided to change his position that Messi really came into his own.

The coach decided that he'd fare better playing as an inside attacking midfielder (better named as a false number 9) instead of on the wings.

Guardiola wrote in his book "Herr Pep," that the moment Messi switched positions with Samuel Eto'o (his teammate at Barcelona) was the moment Barcelona turned a 0–0 game against Real Madrid upside down. That game ended with a 6–2 humiliating defeat against their biggest enemy, and in their own stadium, the Santiago Bernabéu.

The best strikers can, and should, take on different roles. You may be familiar with Wayne Rooney and have likely seen him dominating on the field whenever he plays deep in the middle.

Well, there's more to Rooney than first meets the eye. Despite being a pure center forward, he has also played in every single position in Manchester United's front. Rooney hasn't just played in different positions, but he's performed exceptionally well in them too.

The Togolese forward, Emmanuel Adebayor, also has Wayne Roony's multitasking skills. Adebayor came to Arsenal a couple of years before Thierry Henry left to play for Barcelona.

Here he played as a second striker, and sometimes in the middle as an attacking midfielder. After Henry`s departure, Adebayor moved to the position of center forward. Again, he excelled in his new role. In fact, he took to it like a duck takes to water.

Aside from playing in your permanent position, you should also be flexible enough to switch roles whenever there's a need. Such times might include when the ball is not yours but you're better placed to take it.

Another is when you find a better location to receive the ball than your own domain. Maybe you get an opportunity to create danger for the rival side by changing positions. These situations and more besides should always be open for consideration.

The main weak point of any defensive player, no matter how skilled he is, or how rough he might play, is that he can't see with his back. This is your edge, providing you know how to use it.

The moment a defender looks around for the ball, or for you, is the exact moment to seize an opportunity when there is one. You might do this by finding a new space for yourself or by switching positions with another teammate.

This quick thinking is only effective if your teammate understands your intentions. In other words, you are both on the same page. Your lines of communication are open, even though you might not utter a word to each other.

Great strikers are flexible, versatile, and most importantly, they are communicative. They work as "part of" their team and not "apart from" their team.

31. Not Being a Good Finisher

A good striker, is a good finisher, is a good striker.

The one major skill, and the most important attribute for any striker, is his ability to finish. A striker's success is gaged by how many goals he can score (average per game) and his seasonal total.

Whether he plays on the wings or as a center forward, it really doesn't matter. What matters most when evaluating how good or bad he is, and how much money a club should pay for him, is his record and potential.

The definition of a good striker is one who keeps scoring goals. As long as you can smash the ball into the net, and as long as you are doing it with predicable frequency, nobody cares too much about anything else you can do. Okay, that's not quite true, but everything else takes second priority to goal scoring.

The only way to turn yourself into a goal-scoring machine, and to maintain consistency, is to work on your finishing skills.

Case Study: Arsenal`s front line up

At the time of writing, Arsenal's attacking line includes the following players:

- Olivier Giroud
- Theo Walcott
- Danny Welbeck
- Lukas Podolski
- Yaya Sanogo

All the five names mentioned above play in front of one of the most magical and most assisting attacking midfielders that any striker can dream of having on his side.

I am of course talking about the German Mesut Özil. Özil is one of Europe`s most talented playmakers, in addition to the fabulous trio Aaron Ramsey, Santi Cazorla and Jack Wilshere.

Unfortunately, not one of the five Arsenal players above is any good at finishing. In fact, Giroud - the best among them - has an average goal scoring record of just 19 goals per season.

This number is achievable in one quarter of a season by a strong finisher like Messi or Cristiano, or even Luis Suarez.

Believe me when I say this: If you can leverage your skills and become an excellent finisher, then your success is in the bag, guaranteed, no matter what.

Two Steps to Becoming a Good Finisher

To become a lethal finisher requires only two things: a good eye and controlled aggression.

You need to have a good eye for spotting opportunities that others are likely to miss. This is yet another skill that you can develop with the right tools and guidance. Reading the game will be your first biggest asset.

Having the mental determination to follow through comes next. If you fail to see the less obvious opportunities, then you can't possibly act on them. This is why it's crucial that you develop a good eye for these things.

You also need to have an aggressive, no mercy, take no prisoner attitude to succeed at finishing. This is no time for pleasantries.

Nor can you hesitate. This is an almost primitive survival instinct that has to take root in your psyche. Your aggression needs to be there always, waiting to spring into action the moment you call on it.

Understanding the Mind

Your brain needs to have controlled aggression programmed within it. It should send a direct signal to your feet to direct the ball in any direction you choose.

You finish without giving anything too much thought. You intuitively know what needs doing and the rest, as they say, is history.

Note that ability without faith is futile. The only way to score goals, and to be consistent at scoring goals, is to believe you can do it 110%.

Knowing you can finish, and believing you can finish, is not the same thing. Let's look at an example of this.

Maybe you can perform something with total precision and skill when the pressure is off. However, when the pressure is on, you go to pieces trying to perform that exact same action. This tells you two things.

The first thing it tells you is that you can definitely perform the action. After all, you've done it a thousand times before without any problems.

The second thing it tells you is that you can't perform that action under pressure, no matter how hard you try.

The conclusion is this: You have the physical ability but not the faith to carry it out when it matters most.

This is why developing the right mindset is so important when it comes to finishing. If your brain says "NO" then you have zero chance until you can switch your thinking.

Don't forget too, a striker's finishing moments are often actions performed alone. There is probably not going to be anyone around to assist you at that final dash for the goal. This means you have to believe in yourself before going in for the kill.

You must be tough and you must be rough if that's what the situation calls for, but in a sporty way of course. You need to play as if your life depends on it.

Get into that mode and you have some idea of how determined you need to be in those final moments.

In fact, you need to be more machine than man when you're going in hard. It sounds tough because it is tough, at least in a lot of cases, but the more you do it, the more resilient you will become.

Some things, more so than others, need repeating over and over before they get to sink in. The importance of embracing the right mindset is one of those things.

I will keep talking about the "mental game," and how to modify your way of thinking as we go through the remainder of this book.

Reaching success in soccer, like any other sport come to that, is all about having the right belief system. Before you can believe, you first have to have the right attitude, an open mind, and a balanced outlook. If it all sounds too much, fear not.

You can train the mind just like you can train any part of the physical body. All you need is a good understanding of how to think and the right tools make those changes. If you have a genuine determination to achieve your objectives, then you will be triumphant.

To quote the wise words of Dr. Wayne Dyer: "Change the way you look at things, and the things you look at change."

As mentioned in an earlier chapter, the key to success is to think successful thoughts. In your case, this means thinking BIG.

Small actions will deliver small results, just as big actions will yield much greater returns. What you put in to something determines what you get out of it. It really is as simple as that.

Your mind and body have to be in sync. If they don't talk to each other, or they talk in different dialects, then you're on a hiding to nothing from the off. To illustrate this point I will use a hypothetical situation.

He Who Dares Wins

Someone is standing at the edge of a very tall bridge overlooking white water rapids a long way below them. They've paid to do a bungee jump, yet when the time comes to take that leap of faith their mind locks up.

It won't let them go, no matter how much they know they are physically capable of performing the jump.

That's how influential the mind can be. It has the potential to control your physical actions, or inactions, and all your final decisions.

In the scenario above, our friend chickened out at the last minute because their mind told them to. In the meantime, one jumper after another threw themselves off that bridge. The nervous one was left sitting to one side watching everyone else have the time of their life.

Dare to Win

To be a successful and fearless striker, you cannot let your mind control you. It is you who has to control your mind. Your mind belongs to you; you do not belong to it.

It is there for you to use as and when you call on it. You are not your mind; your mind is simply a part of your being.

Whenever you want to do something but can't do it, that is the mind taking control of your decisions. Even though you might think you have made a conscious decision, you haven't, not really; your mind has decided for you.

If you can identify with any of this, don't worry, it's not a fault, or at least it's not your fault. It has come about by years of subconscious conditioning.

Most people are not even aware of just how much their mind controls their everyday thoughts and actions.

Just know that your mind can be re-trained, or re-programmed. This is no different to anything else in that once you get to identify the problem, you then set about working on the solution (fix).

You Still Need Aggression

Aggression will force you to go for every ball, every pass and every cross. It will make you take advantage of every mistake and erratic ball that comes into play.

Only aggression and a strong work ethic will set you apart from your peers. It will perceive you as a formidable force on the soccer field.

Aggression isn't simply about being tough. You can be strong and bullish under normal circumstances yet timid on the field.

Once again, this is something that relates back to mindset and how you perceive yourself. It's not a case of is there aggression within you, it's more a case of can you let it out when you need it.

Aggression in Perspective

It's important to put aggression into perspective. Most people think of aggression as feelings of anger or antipathy, resulting in hostile or violent behavior. This is actually uncontrolled aggression and has no place on the soccer field.

What you need is "controlled aggression." This means you have a readiness to attack or confront with force and determination, but in a controlled fashion. There is no time for good manners or hesitation on the soccer field.

In fact, there might even be casualties as you charge toward the goal, although this is neither your concern nor your intention. If your opponents do experience a little bruising along the way then so be it.

When you can channel aggressive play into your finishing style, your fans, your coach and your teammates will respect your for it. Even if you fail to score, everyone notices and respects a good effort.

Center forwards who try their best, and half kill themselves with every ball, get so much more respect over lazy strikers.

Those who play it safe and hold back for easy opportunities never get too far in their soccer careers.

Goals, Not Style, Preside

In the above section we looked at channeled aggression. When it comes to soccer, this is a type of aggression which converts into positive, productive actions on the field.

In the case of a good striker, his channeled aggression is most evident when he's attempting to finish. Channeled aggression means it's controlled, that you're in control.

The problem that many strikers have is that they go in too hard when it's not necessary. Too much aggression and speed at the wrong time is a surefire way to lose focus and control.

Channeling the right about of aggression into the right situation is a skill that can only come about by experience.

Some strikers like to go in hard whether it's necessary or not, just to make an impression. Others like to score using some fancy moves. Too much or too little of anything is a recipe for failure.

Sure it's nice to score with an impressive finish, but it should never be your main aim. The only thing that matters to your team, your coach, and your fans, is whether your score or not.

Goals have to be your primary focus – always! A dull, slow ball rolling into the back of the net is still a goal and better than an impressive shot that never makes it.

If showing off is your thing, and seeking personal glory, then you will never make the grade of a top striker.

There will always be situations that need impressive shots to score goals, without you having to create them. Control is your key weapon.

A striker will sometimes lose great goal scoring opportunities because he felt the need to do something fancy with the ball. Whenever this happens, he has just lost his control and core focus.

The lesson to take from this is to never lose sight of your principal aim, which is to score goals using whatever way warrants it at the time.

Keep this central in your mind and you will remain grounded and consistent. To do this you need to take yourself out of the equation and think of the broader team effort over your own ego.

Losing Confidence

You will experience good days and bad days on the field, as we all do. When things are not going your way there is a potential for losing your confidence. This is a trap that you have to learn to avoid at all costs.

The secret for maintaining confidence is to live in the moment. The way to stay in the "now," as I like to call it, is to ignore the noise that might be going on inside your head.

What happens when you're not doing so well is that you fear things getting even worse. This means you're thinking about other potential disasters that may lie ahead.

In other words, you have too much "future" occupying your mind. This creates feelings of unease, anxiety, tension, and worry. You can't possibly focus on the here and now when your mind is elsewhere.

The second you identify any loss of confidence, is the moment you have to switch your focus back to the present. The best way to do that is to get back into the game and concentrate your mind on what's important.

Just know that there are only two options open to you when faced with a negative situation. Once is to accept things and move on with the game, and the other is to deal with it, if that's still an option. That's it, acceptance or fresh action.

Remember, "now" is the only time you have. What is done is done and it cannot be undone. Everything happens in the "now" so make sure every one of your "now moments" counts as you go forward.

32. Not Being Relaxed in Front of the Goal

Case Study: The Relaxed Dutch Vs. Argentina

Dennis Bergkamp is a former Dutch striker who played for both Arsenal and Inter Milan. He was one of the most skilled and most underrated strikers in the history of modern soccer. He was also one of the most composed as well.

This was a man who never tried to hide his fear of flying, yet he wasn't a nervous person in general. His flying phobia materialized after an engine cut out during a flight to the USA 94 World Cup.

It was an experience that left the Holland international afraid to take to the air ever again. Other than his refusal to take to the skies, Bergkamp remains one of the calmest soccer players I have ever seen.

His goal against Argentina in the quarterfinal game of the 1998 World Cup was an excellent demonstration of his composed manner. He maintained an immense and deep sense of calmness in front of the goal when all around his was frantic. He seemed to casually tap the ball into the net as if it were no big deal, without any real need to rush.

Search on YouTube for "The legendary World Cup goal from Dennis Bergkamp" and you will see exactly what I'm talking about. In the clip you see him receive a long ball from Frank de Boer.

He then gets the ball under his control, in his own time, before then glancing up at the keeper and then BAM! He scores. The Dutch commentator at the time goes absolutely crazy with excitement.

This all happened in the 89th minute of the game. Even though time was running out, and the Dutch side was up against a big team in an important game, Bergkamp remained unflustered. What a classic this goal was, and one that will have its place in the "best ever goals" Hall of Fame.

Bergkamp's style of calm composed playing was not a one-off event. In fact, just one year previous he scored a similar goal against Leicester City. It was the same through-ball, the same excellent ball control, and the same unhurried, controlled approach. The keeper didn't stand a chance.

This is not a style of play that suites everyone. In fact, some players could never be so calm in such hectic situations, no matter how much they practiced at it. It's like I've pointed out throughout this book, once you get to master various skills, you will then go on to develop your own unique style of play.

This calm, composed approach by Bergkamp is his style. It doesn't mean he's not all fired up inside and hungry to succeed. It just means he's able to channel his energy and somewhat latent aggression into a slower, more carefully calculated style of play.

When asked if there was any secret behind his composed manner, Bergkamp said that meditation helped him a lot. Now, just because meditation helps him, that doesn't mean it is right for someone else.

It might be, but it won't necessarily be. We all need to find our own tools to experiment with, things that work best for us personally.

In Bergkamp's book "Stillness and Speed: My Story," he writes about how meditating helped him to maintain a relaxed demeanor, both on and off the field. He would practice every day. In fact, it was part of his early morning ritual.

The competitive world of soccer can be intense at times, that's for sure. We often witness players who lose their cool in a moment of madness. However, when aggression manifests itself in anger and resentment, the one who loses out is the one who's fuming.

When composure is lost in this way it can be hard to regain focus and control. When that happens, it obviously has a negative impact on the player.

You can still play a fast and fiercely competitive game while remaining calm inside. All the best decisions happen when a striker is living in the moment. He knows exactly what he's doing and about to do. At that moment, nothing or nobody is in a position to distract him.

You might want to try meditation for yourself. It is only by trying different things that you get to find out what works for you and what doesn't. Meditation doesn't need any special skills or occupational qualifications.

It doesn't require any special equipment either. In other words, you have nothing to lose by giving it a go other than a few minutes of your time.

If it all sounds a bit too "spiritual" for you, and not your thing, then try to view it in a different way. Look at meditation as nothing more than sitting still in a quiet space for a set period of time.

After all, that's what it is in its most basic form. Set aside just 15-30 minutes a day for a week, and at the same time each day. You will know by the end of your seven day trial whether you want to carry on or not.

Those who gain from meditation say it enhances their focus and increases their awareness. Meditation is also supposed to lessen any sense of fear. Any reduction in fear and apprehension will help you to play better soccer under pressure.

How to Meditate

- Wear something loose-fitting and comfortable.
- Find a calm space to practice.
- Switch off your mobile and any other distracting devices.
- Get into a comfortable sitting position with your feet resting flat on the floor.

- Close your eyes and focus on your breath, breathing in through your nose and out through the mouth.
- Stay put for the time you have set aside.
- Let any thoughts come and go from your mind. Try not to control them or get into internal conversations. Just allow them to happen. Your aim here is to just watch your thoughts as an outside observer.

The above guide is the most basic level of meditation. If you feel you want to get into this more seriously, then there is a plethora of great advice out there on the web.

33. Not Noticing the Keeper`s Position when Shooting

Something that will help to boost your goal finishing approach is to keep a firm eye on the position of the goalkeeper. Knowing where he is just before you shoot will make your shots easier and more accurate.

As you prepare for your shot you need to establish the angle you'll be firing from. You also need to be sure of the ball's range.

Make a quick mental note of the keeper's potential to stretch or dive to save or intercept your ball. All these quick observations are crucial for your success when playing on the front line. Anything else is just potluck.

A goalkeeper actually has quite a limited toolkit at his disposal. This is despite being able to use his hands to defend the goal.

Even the best goalkeepers like Buffon or Cech, have a limited diving range and limited reflexes. When dealing with strong, accurate shots there is only so much a goalie can do.

Just like field players, goalkeepers also have their strong and weak points. As a striker it always pays to study the goalies that you'll be up against before the game.

If you get the chance to see vids of these keepers in advance, then it will definitely give you an edge. Viewing video footage can help to enhance and sharpen the way you play on the day.

Knowing where the keeper is before taking aim is obviously to your best advantage. Knowing how he might react to your shot is going to help you even more.

I like to talk a lot about the retired French forward Thierry Henry, and for good reason. Henry is perhaps the best attacking player ever to have played in the English premier league.

Not only was the man a true goal scoring machine, but he also had class and style to boot. These are qualities which are hard to find these days.

One of Henry`s greatest goals, perhaps even his best ever goal, was against Manchester United at Highbury.

This was a game where Arsenal triumphed with a 1–0 victory. In this goal, Henry received a pass on the edge of Man United`s penalty area. He had his back facing the keeper at the time and was surrounded by two of United`s defenders.

What happened next?

Henry, chipped the ball a few centimeters above the ground (back still facing the goal), and assisted the ball to himself.

Then, and without even looking at the goal or the keeper, he placed a chip over Fabian Bartez (Manchester United's keeper), which landed right at the top left corner of United`s goal. It was amazing.

To summarize this chapter: Increase your chances of scoring by running quick scenarios over in your head before taking a shot at the goal. You need to work out where the keeper is in relation to yourself.

If you can get to know a bit about his style of play before the game, then do so.

Make these things a natural part of your preparation and style and see your game move up a level. The better you prepare, the better you play.

34. Not Messing with the Goalkeeper

Case Study: Artur Boruc at the Emirates

Make sure you stay close to the goalkeeper right after corners and before punts. There will always be occasions when a goalie is not aware of your presence. When this happens, he might just put the ball on the ground; often to his detriment.

Some keepers start to punt the ball next to where you're standing, although they don't know it. When this happens, it leaves an open invitation for you to slip the ball away from right under their nose.

There have been many goals scored this way in the past, and there will be many more in the future. This is why you should always prepare to mess with the keeper.

I once watched a game between English teams Arsenal (the Gunners) and Southampton (The Saints). It was in the Emirates stadium.

This was the last game for the Saints` goalkeeper Artur Boruc, who was 33 at the time. He never made it to the starting lineup and spent the rest of his days on the bench because of one incident.

What happened?

The Saints (who were third on the league table at the time) were playing a good game against the Gunners. In actual fact, they were attacking hard, but they wasted a couple of potential goals.

It all went wrong for the Saints when one of their defenders sent the ball toward goalkeeper Boruc. Unfortunately, Boruc began to panic.

He then hesitated before attempting to dribble Arsenal`s striker Olivier Giroud. Giroud had no difficulty stealing the ball from the Polish goalie at all. Once he got by Boruc, he went on to score an easy goal for his team.

The best thing about this goal was Giroud`s aggression and fast response. You could see his willingness to play for every ball and look out for every opportunity going.

In this case, he found an opening and went in for the kill; something which panicked Boruc. The keeper hesitated for just a second and Giroud spotted that and seized the moment.

If Giroud hadn't pressured the keeper with his fast, aggressive attack, then the keeper might not have panicked and hesitated as he did.

You can see what influence you can have on the keepers, and other players, just by having the right approach at the right moment. Without pressuring the keeper to make the mistake, Giroud probably wouldn't have scored.

One of the biggest oversights made by a lot of strikers is their failure to pressure goalkeepers, or to mess with them in some way. Try not to fall into this trap.

Tactical aggression is a great asset for strikers, as is a cheeky sneakiness, like hovering around a keeper to his unawares.

Anything you can do to startle a goalie, scare him, or cause him to lose focus in some way, is going to pay off.

Case Study: The "Henry / Friedel" incident.

This is an incident that occurred in a game with Arsenal playing against Blackburn Rovers. The French forward, Thierry Henry, shadowed the Rover's goalkeeper, Brad Friedel, after a corner.

Henry waited until the American keeper let go of the ball to punt it. Just as the ball was midair, Henry stole if from the keeper and went on to score an easy goal for his side.

It was a beautiful goal by Henry but for some reason the referee decided to disallow it.

This was a controversial decision because the ref was far away from the play.

Worse still was that he didn't even consult his linesman. Anyone who has seen that goal will agree that it was 100% accurate and the ref should never have withdrawn it.

Anyway, despite the dispute, this move from Henry was still pure genius. This is another prime example of why you should stick around the goal area and expect keeper slip-ups. After all, if you're not there, you can't seize the opportunities as and when they arise.

35. Missing on Easy Balls

All goalkeepers make mistakes, and they make a lot of them too, fortunately for you. It's the nature of the position. Smart, attacking players are the ones who can predict, and successfully exploit, goalkeeper mistakes.

Here are a few of the more typical blunders made by goalies: Missed passes, dropped balls, an uncovered near post, an uncovered angle, advancing too far outside the goal.

Perhaps one of the biggest blunders a goalie can make is to put the ball on the ground without being aware of your presence in the penalty area. This can, and often does happen, so make sure you're always ready to pounce.

The above mistakes are pretty typical for a lot of goalies. The thing is that nobody is in a better position to exploit them than a smart striker. He is the one who's most mindful of such blunders and ready to act at a moment's notice.

There are also plenty of less switched-on strikers who overlook typical keeper errors. Make sure you don't become one of them. Seriously, there are some easy goals to come out of goalkeeper slips. The saying: "Never look a gift horse in the mouth," springs to mind.

Case Study: Gonzalo Higuaín (Messi`s nightmare)

You may or may not have heard of the Argentine striker Gonzalo Higuaín. Anyway, he's the guy who currently plays for S.S.C. Napoli and the Argentina national team (at the time of writing). He's also a former Real Madrid striker who scored 122 goals between 2006 and 2013.

Here's what happened during the 2014 World Cup final game between Argentina and Germany. Tony Kroos, the German midfielder, sent a header by mistake to Higuaín.

This pass put him in a one-to-one situation with Germany`s goalkeeper, Manuel Neuer. It was one of those chance encounters that don't happen often in professional soccer.

What did Higuaín do?

It's more a case of what he didn't do that was the problem. He lost a golden opportunity to score. He rushed the ball without taking his time to assess where the keeper and the goal was in relation to himself. He didn`t even take a few steps closer to the goal to secure a better chance of scoring.

Instead he smashed the ball as hard as he could kick as soon as he got it, and from the top of the penalty area too.

He was far away from the German goal, so it wasn't surprising when he missed. No thanks to Higuaín, Argentina lost the chance to win their first World Cup in 28 years.

After yet more poor performances, Higuaín popularity went from bad to worse. Many of the Argentina fans hate to see him play for their national team.

Some even call him "the nightmare of Messi," since he's always the man who destroys Messi's hopes of winning his first big trophy with the club.

Here's another incident that shows Higuaín's consistency to fail. This time it was during the Copa America championship. This is a competition that Argentina hasn't won since 1993. Here Argentina was playing in the final game against the host team Chile.

The game was at a 0–0 draw and in the last minutes of extra time. The Argentine forward, Ezequiel Lavezzi, sent a fantastic through-pass to Higuaín, who was just a few inches away from the goal. Once again, Higuaín managed to turn an easy opportunity into a total disaster.

In this case, the result was a goal kick instead of a goal, but it didn't end there. He made things even worse by wasting his ball in the penalty shootout, thus helping Chile to win its first Copa America title ever.

There are other high-profile mistakes too. Because of these slipups, Higuaín has lost most of his credibility and reputation for wasting easy opportunities by his silly, and quite unnecessary, blunders.

What he fails to do, and what you should take from his failures, is that he doesn't learn from his past mistakes.

If you don't learn from them, then you go on to repeat more of the same. Consistency in failed attempts is not good for anyone.

Remember, mistakes are part of the learning process. We even welcome the occasional blunders when they make us stronger.

However, if they don't make us stronger, they either prevent us from progressing with our development, or they make us weaker.

Retired Argentine striker, Martin Palermo, wasted three penalties in a single game against Colombia. He did this by opting to aim all three shots at the middle of the goal. One of his attempts even went off into sky.

He made a joke of himself at the time, though deep inside I doubt he thought it was funny. I bet none of his teammates was laughing either. The other players would never forget his idiotic mistake, how could they possibly?

But it has to be the penalty taker who suffers the most. When something like this happens to a player, it just has to dent his self-confidence.

In fact, such a blunder as three missed penalties in a single game is enough to demoralize anyone, and with potentially long lasting effects too.

We all have our bad days as well as our good days, but when there's a bad- bad day, then something's not quite right.

The importance of staying on top of your game cannot be stressed often enough. Now I don't know the full story behind Palermo, but this did not look like a man who was in control at the time.

One missed penalty from a professional soccer player should have made him pause, recompose himself, and rethink his strategy before having another go.

He should have tried something different but he didn't. He failed to learn from the mistakes of the previous, failed attempt, and so he got more of the same – twice more!

The moral of this story is that you can learn from the mistakes of others as well as those of your own. This brings us on nicely to the next chapter, "Not Practicing Penalties."

36. Not Practicing
Penalties

One of the best soccer players to ever play in the English premier league was a guy by the name of Matt Le Tissier.

Guernsey-born Matt Le Tissier, spent 16 years of his career playing for his beloved Southampton. Although he's now retired, the Le Tissier's legacy lives on.

He was an attacking midfielder with exceptional technical skills. He was the second highest scorer for Southampton behind striker Mick Channon.

Le Tissier was the Professional Footballers' Association (PFA) Young Player of the Year in 1990. He was also the first midfielder to score 100 goals in the Premier League. His record at scoring penalty kicks was phenomenal, scoring, from the spot, 47 times out of 48 attempts.

He was what you can call a complete player. Le Tissier was a wonderful passer and he had a good vision.

His ability to read the game kept him forever consistent. Even to this day, he has one of the best shooting techniques you will ever witness.

I recommend that you spend some time watching Le Tissier`s videos. Look especially for any footage that shows his shooting style.

You will soon see why the man was a true premier league legend, and no one would ever doubt that. However, this is not a chapter on the life and times of Matt Le Tissier. If you haven't already guessed, we are going to look closer at his superb penalty taking skills.

Thirteen years after he retired, Le Tissier still holds the highest penalty scoring ratio in the history of the English premier league.

Le Tissier`s penalty ratio of 96.15% is even better than all the other premier league legends. Some of these include Thierry Henry (92 %), Alan Shearer (83.58 %) Wayne Rooney (68.15 %), and Manchester United`s wonderful trio; Roy Keane, Ryan Giggs and David Beckham.

Even payers with natural talent know that they will not be able to perform under pressure unless they maintain their performance levels.

Le Tissier wasn't a top scorer because he was great at shooting. He was great at shooting because he made himself that way.

What you see on the field is a tiny fraction of what goes on in the life of a soccer superstar. Most of the grunt work and determined effort goes on behind the scenes, away from the public eye.

I'm mentioning Le Tissier as a way to remind you of the importance of practicing and mastering the art of taking penalties. You never know when your turn might come.

Honestly, could you think of any worse humiliation than being the team's rusty penalty taker? It doesn't bare thinking about.

Too many players nowadays focus on improving their core performance (which is great by the way), but they neglect some of the smaller skills. These are the things that will make you complete. Getting good at scoring penalties is one of those skills you really need to master.

Take a look at the best two players in the world right now, namely Cristiano Ronaldo and Lionel Messi. Both of these guys are exceptional at taking penalties.

Like everything else, practice is the only way to improve. As you know, the more you practice, the more you will excel in the areas that you work on the most. So how is your penalty taking skill?

If you haven't given this much attention in the past, now is the time to change all that. Set yourself some time each day to practice. Try for at least 50 or even 100 penalties shots per session.

Aim to keep them high, keep them strong, and keep them at an angle. This is what we call the perfect or the ideal penalty shot.

After a while, and only once you can see some marked improvements, it's time to ratchet things up a bit. This is the time to start practicing penalties while under pressure.

The Easy Way to Maintain Focus When Playing Penalties

In case you're not familiar with how basketball players practice free throws, here's a quick rundown. Basketball players practice their free throws while someone else is trying to distract them. This might be with a whistle or a buzzer, or any other distraction method that's available.

Basketball players invite distraction for a reason. For these guys, the more distraction there is, the more they welcome it, and why?

Because it teaches them how to cut out external noise and focus on what's most important. For them, the most important thing is their shot at the basket. For a soccer striker, it's his attempts at the goal.

Obviously you can't just click your fingers and have a massive crowd appear to watch you practice your penalty shots. This means you need to get the pressure from something else.

This is where I suggest you take a similar approach to the basketball players. Once you get enough distraction going on around you, you'll definitely experience pressure.

I'm sure you can think of something, but to get your started here's an idea. Ask a friend or teammate to stand close by as you're taking your penalties.

They might blow whistles, wave arms about, shout and scream, or whatever else. Amid all this distraction, try to cut out the noise and focus on performing perfect, high, strong penalties.

I know it all sounds a bit silly, and you will probably have a hard time containing your laughter to begin with. Whatever you do, just hold in there. I can promise you that there is a method behind this madness.

Once you learn to cut out all external distractions and focus solely on your penalty kicks, then you have taken your penalty scoring ability up to a whole new level.

37. Not Practicing Enough Fouls

The most valuable strikers are complete. This means they are successful at penalties, headers, long shots, dribbling, sprinting, reading plays, taking fouls and leadership.

As you can see from the above, the complete attacker can do many different things, and do them well. He can take on different roles, play in different positions, and perform the unexpected. It's all part of being "complete."

The German goalkeeper, Manuel Neuer, once said: "A keeper who`s able to do different things on the field, in addition to what's expected of him between the three bars, is complete."

Any soccer player who can excel, not only at in his main role, but also in other areas of the game, is obvious more valued that one who cannot.

A part of being a complete striker is having the ability to take free kicks from any place on the field. In fact, you must practice at becoming exceptional at taking free kicks if you want to stand out.

Case Study: Juninho Pernambucano

Brazilian player, Juninho Pernambucano, more commonly known as Juninho, is a retired midfielder. He is famous for his bending free kicks. This is a man regarded as the greatest free-kick specialist of all time.

Pernambucano helped his team, Olympique Lyonnais, dominate French soccer. With his help, they went on to win seven consecutive league titles besides seven domestic cups.

There is no question of doubt that Pernambucano is one of the best free-kick takers to have ever played in French professional soccer.

Pernambucano was so great that he had the Italian legend Andrea Pirlo spend a lot of his own time trying to discover the secret behind his excellence.

Pirlo was desperate to know how Pernambucano scored difficult fouls from so many different angles, especially those from awkward positions (something I will reveal later).

Look up "Juninho Pernambucano" on YouTube and search for his top free-kicks. You will get to witness how he would shoot and score from the toughest angles and the farthest positions.

When a player like this can make something so tough look so easy, then you know he's a true master at what he does.

Among his peers, Pernambucano was the top scorer, free-kick taker of them all. He achieved more than 70 goals from free kicks in his illustrious career. This is a number that even phenomenal players like Messi or Ronaldo haven`t even come close to.

In Andrea Pirlo's book "I Think Therefore I Play," Pirlo uncovers the Brazilian`s secret.

It took him many weeks of trial and error to find out, but he eventually discovered what made Pernambucano such a great player. It was, in fact, all down to one simple trick. Drum roll please...

Pernambucano would always keep his foot straight, striking the ball from underneath using only the first three toes of his foot before releasing the ball toward the goal. That's it.

I've said it before and I will say it again: it is often the little things in soccer than can make the biggest difference. Pernambucano had no magic formula up his sleeve.

He had no special bodily functions that the rest of are without. He just had a technique, and one which he mastered with extreme precision.

38. Not Absorbing the Ball when Receiving It

When receiving the ball you must make sure that it won't stray far from your feet. This is the ABC of becoming a successful striker.

There will be many times when you don't have a lot of space to play with the ball. This is because hungry defenders will be buzzing around you like bees to a honeypot. As you know only too well, opponents are super eager to steal that ball from you at the first given opportunity.

This is why the ball must stay close to your feet. As soon as you receive a pass, your job is to absorb the energy of the ball so that it becomes like a natural extension of your foot.

This is the only way you can get the ball under your control right away.

Two Golden Rules for Receiving a Pass

Rule 1: Always direct the ball to the direction you want to take.

You direction may be a new space, or in the direction of a nearby teammate who you want to send the ball to. It doesn't matter where. What matters most is that whenever you receive a pass you remain confident. Most slip-ups occur because of too much hesitation or self-doubt.

Confidence in your ability to perform the next move is fundamental to your success in any play. Know where you want to direct the ball and make your move.

Playing calm doesn't mean you have to play slow. It just means that you're in control and you know what you need to do next, and have the confidence to carry that out.

Good skills coupled with quick, accurate action will save you time. Oftentimes, playing this way will also surprise the one marking you and send him off balance.

In short, keep one step ahead of the game at all times and be prepared.

Rule 2: Always move towards the ball.

Here we touch on the hesitation trap again. Even a lost second or two can break your plans.

Don't wait for the pass to reach you, move toward the ball whenever possible. You need to do this so that you can prevent the man marking you from intercepting the pass before it reaches you.

By meeting the ball half way, you are also escaping the defender who's marking you.

Furthermore, your move will make him chase after you if he's doing his job properly. This will then create extra space for any attacking teammate who's coming up from behind.

39. Lacking Confidence in Your Own Skills

As I've said before, confidence is the key to your success. It will not only make you fearless, but it will also make your defenders fearful of you.

No matter what happens during a game, you must remain confident. Even if your performance is suffering on the day, you can't let it get to you. If you don't feel assertive, then at least convey confidence.

This way your opponents don't get to feed off your uncertainty. If you need to fake confidence, then fake it, right up until the last play and the final whistle.

A lot of strikers don't put enough emphasis on the psychological game of soccer, but they should do. Make sure you don't fall into this trap. The game against your opponent's is as much about mind games as it is about physical ability.

Do whatever is necessary to keep your opponents guessing and out of the game. Remember to maintain a confident manner at all times. Portray a positive stance, even if you don't feel particularly positive. If you can find any way to distract or talk your opponent out of his focus then do it, without hesitation.

The striker's role is one where you must show leadership skills. To be a true leader you have to have confidence, faith and aggression.

Okay, so this might be easier to say than it is to do, especially if you're getting a hiding from the rival side. Still, a losing run is no excuse to let your guard down.

You need to keep your spirits up by playing a positive and assertive game, under all conditions. This is what truly separates the men from the boys.

There have been some remarkable comebacks in soccer games over the years, and there always will be. You have to believe that anything is still possible, no matter how far behind you might be trailing. Giving up should never be an option, not ever!

Remember that positivity is infectious, just as negativity can be. If you lose enthusiasm - and it shows - this can have a knock-on effect to the rest of the team. This is why nobody likes to be around weak players.

Those who give up without a fight will never be valued members of any soccer team. Whenever you feel like tutting, puffing, rolling back the eyes, or displaying other negative form or body language, try doing the opposite instead. Look fired up, enthusiastic, and hungry for battle. Shout excitedly and motivate the players. Let them know that nothing is over until that final whistle blows.

All the famous strikers are convincing. They show strong character and have a kind of aura around them that radiates positivity.

These are the guys who have that "winning mentality" that prevents them from surrendering. They always bounce back, refusing to stay down and concede defeat until the referee ends the game.

As I've already pointed out, there will be times when things just aren't going your way. Sometimes your team will play so bad that you will lose the will to go on. Other times it will be you who's the weak link in the chain.

In either scenario, you should pause for a moment, take stock, and press the reset button. In other words, you can restart the game anytime you want to. When nothing seems to be going right, never accept things as they are. Change is always an option.

Now, let's just say that despite your best effort to motivate the team, they just can't seem to get their act together.

This doesn't mean you also have to give up. It is still your responsibility to play at your best and do what you can for the side. After all, your name, your reputation and your enjoyment are still important.

Leadership Matters

In all areas of life, not just soccer, there are basically two kinds of people. We have leaders and we have foot soldiers.

Worth noting here is that both types of people are equally as important as each other for things to run smoothly. Both leaders and foot soldiers need each other.

We can't all be leaders, and nor could everyone function as a foot soldiers. As a striker, you will either have natural leadership qualities or you will need to develop them.

Your role is to motivate and to delegate, and how well or how poor you do this will often determine the outcome of a game.

Maybe you're looking to make a full time career in soccer. On the other hand, perhaps you just want to be a valuable asset to your beloved local team.

Whichever it is, force yourself to be that guy who leads others and emits a positive air to those around him. Such players are a rare breed.

This is why they are extremely valuable to any team, amateur and professional alike. Be that one.

40. Needing Too Much Space to Prepare for Shoots

Smart Strikers make use of the only space they get.

Bruce Lee, the Kung Fu master, had a famous trick up his sleeve.

It was his infamous one inch punch. In fact, there has never been a feat of martial arts that is more impressive than his famous short strike.

This was an action which allowed Lee to make a powerful and effective move from just one inch away. Best of all is that he didn't need any space to prepare for this lethal hit.

What's this got to do with soccer, I hear you say. Well, this same concept is what you have to do with the ball.

The less space and time you use to generate enough power to make an effective shot, the more effective and feared you will become as a player.

Watch Cristiano Ronaldo's shooting style and you will see what I'm talking about. Note how the Real Madrid attacker rarely moves the ball away from his feet before taking a shot. This is particularly evident when defenders from both sides surround him.

This fast-acting skill is more important to strikers than it is to midfielders and playmakers.

This is because they have enough space outside the penalty area to generate the power to strike.

This is a luxury that attackers just don't have. They usually have to act real fast and try to send that ball to the goal before a defender gets chance to intercept it.

Having the ability to perfect and perform shots in tight spaces will be a real asset to you.

This is one of the strong points of the Polish striker, Robert Lewandowski. He's able to shoot from any place, in any condition, using his right foot, his left foot and his head.

Although Lewandowski can be a bit heavy on the ground, his other skills make up for any shortcomings he might have.

His ability to shoot in tight spaces, along with his powerful shots and accurate headers, makes him unique. In fact, he's one of the best center forwards in both Europe and the world because of this.

In order to excel, you need to work hard at developing this skill. Once you do get good at it, you will be able pull a lot of rabbits out of the hat when on the field.

41. Not Being Selfish.
Always Wanting for More

I like the way Arjen Robben approaches soccer. This is despite the fact that he's often called selfish by fans and by some of his peers.

Robben, who plays for the German side Bayern Munich, is not always easy to deal with. There are times when the Dutch winger would rather die than pass the ball to a nearby teammate.

One of Robben's famous moves (not typical of most wingers) is to sprint on the right flank. Then, instead of passing the ball on or going for a cross, he goes deeper inside the field. When he thinks the time is right, he sends a strong ball right towards the opposite side of the goal.

In one incident, Robben refused to let his teammate, Thomas Muller, take a penalty. This was despite Muller being the best man for the job. In fact, Thomas Muller happens to be one of the best penalty takers in Germany.

He was also the first player to shoot penalties for Bayern Munich in the extra time of the UEFA Champions league against Chelsea. Yet despite all this, Robben went ahead and took the penalty. The outcome was that he sent a reasonably soft kick right into the hands of Chelsea`s keeper, Petr Čech.

After reading about the selfishness of Arjen Robben, you might now be wondering why I like his style of play.

Well, under normal circumstances there is no room for selfish play in soccer. After all, it is a team sport. That said, the role of a striker is a little different to other positions on the field.

In actual fact, selfishness is one of the key attributes of an A–class striker. That doesn't mean it is necessary at all times, not at all, but there are other times when a striker must play in a selfish way for the good of the team.

It might not always look like the right choice at the time, but a successful outcome can often change opinions on that.

The reason I believe in a little selfish behavior for the striker role is simple. It shows a real hunger and aggression. It's a sign of always wanting more.

Yes, it's a team sport, but sometimes, especially when the pressure is on you to score goals, then a little ball hogging can be the right decision.

You don't need to take my word for it. Look around you and watch the biggest names in the game. The best of the best strikers all show a mix of confidence, bravery and selfishness.

They often try out new moves, new tricks and difficult plays instead of passing the ball. They do this because their chance of succeeding is high, most of the time. If they didn't think they could succeed, then they wouldn't be so selfish on these occasions.

Take Cristiano Ronaldo for example. This is a guy who gets angry whenever he misses a ball or when another Real Madrid attacker touches a ball that was on its way to him.

You can see him getting agitated even when his teammate scores a goal that he thinks should have been his.

Ronaldo's winning mentality and competence is what makes him the master of his own game. He is the one who likes to go for every foul, every penalty and every pass.

If it was up to him, he would be the only player on the field, running rings around the opposition. Well, he might be great, but he's not Barry Allen!

Another example is Alexis Sanchez, the Chilean forward who plays for Arsenal. He also has this selfish streak that he can tap into whenever he feels the moment is appropriate.

He's usually right too.

As you can see, there are times when it is right for a striker to play the selfish card. There are also times when he needs to be a good team player too.

Only experience will help you find that balance.

42. Not Enhancing Your "One Second Acceleration"

There is a useful skill that will help you a lot when dealing with aggressive defenders. It is something I refer to as the "one second acceleration." This is especially useful for dealing with guys who are strong, heavy, tall, and slow on their feet.

What Is the One Second Acceleration?

The 'one second acceleration' is a skill that enables you to get away from a tricky situation fast.

The idea is that you can move with the ball from the standing still position to your fastest speed in the blink of an eye.

It is a move that allows you to escape quickly and pass through any tough defender who's marking you.

To see an example of this, search for Thierry Henry`s famous goal against Inter Milan in a UEFA Champions league game where Arsenal won by 5–1.

You will see how Henry takes the ball 15 meters behind the center line towards Inter's penalty area. Here there were no Inter players to face other than Javier Zanetti.

Henry then goes on to trick him using the skill I'm talking about. In the moment before he shoots, Henry takes the ball from the stationary position before accelerating off at speed.

He then goes on to score an absolutely fantastic goal in the blink of an eye.

A powerful car or a superbike that can accelerate from 0-60 miles an hour in just a few seconds is an impressive sight.

Human acceleration, although slow in comparison to machine, can be equally as impressive.

Just watch the sheer speed that some strikers can reach during a high-paced, game of soccer. It can be jaw dropping at times.

If you don't yet have that 'one second acceleration, you might want to get working on it. If you're already good, then you need to work at becoming even better.

43. Not Owning Your Mistakes

If you have read all the previous chapters, you will know that mistakes can be a great asset to any player. In fact, we learn more from our mistakes than we do our successes, but only when we accept them and act on them. Still not convinced?

OK, let me give you a few more detailed reasons of how failure can be more beneficial to you than success ever could.

To start with, there is nothing to learn from success because we have already succeeded. All we can do with success is attempt to be even more successful by working at it still further.

There are lots of things we can learn from failure though. This is why we should embrace disappointments and setbacks and see what we can take from them.

Failure can reveal your weaknesses and that's really useful to know. It gives you experience and encourages lateral thinking. Failure also encourages the strong and discourages the weak.

It helps to builds character and makes you more intangible / thick-skinned. Failure makes you honest with yourself and encourages improvement & better planning.

As you can see, that's quite a list. To sum up, success is the attitude and failure is the lever. Failure is your friend, so make sure you use it to your best advantage.

The only time a striker, or any other player, learns from his mistakes is when he takes full responsibility for them all. This means every single thing that happens to him, including trivial situations.

When it comes to soccer, it can be the tiniest of things that make the biggest difference. In other words, a small tweak to the way you do something could skyrocket your performance in some area. But unless you can identify and accept any flaws you may have, then you can't apply the solution.

Think of it like this: When you own the problem, you get to be the solution. However, if somebody else is the problem (or the cause of it), you're then into the blame game. When this happens, you have no solution.

If you always fail at a thing because of someone or something else, then you have a role to play in there somewhere. It is your job to find your part and then work at fixing it.

It's too easy to blame some person, some place or some other thing on our failures. This approach is a waste of time and energy, and not at all helpful to us. In fact, "blame" shouldn't even be the word to use as it indicates fault, so it's a bad choice of word.

We're not trying to shame ourselves, or anyone else, by looking for "faults."

What we are doing is discovering those areas of our game which are not working for us. Once we can identify what these are, we can then start working at fixing them.

Remember, there is absolutely nothing wrong with failing. As long as we learn from mistakes and use them to develop our game still further, then our shortcomings become our best assets. This is what we get to do once we embrace failure as a valuable learning tool.

Let's say that after a little digging, you get to realize that you're not fast enough, motivated enough, or strong enough, as three examples. You have just made a great discovery.

You no longer have to blame your shortcomings on the bad weather, the goalkeeper, your coach, or bad luck, etc.

You have discovered that your failure is because of something you are doing or not doing. That's fantastic news. Now that you understand the problem you can start working on the solution.

44. Not Being Familiar with the Laws of the Game

There Is No Offside Count in These Three Cases:

- If the pass was a corner kick.
- If the pass was a throw in.

- If the pass came to you from an opponent (either a field player of the goalkeeper).

Simulations Can Get You into Trouble When:

- You throw yourself to the ground (faking a tackle) in an attempt to get a penalty kick or a serious free kick close to the penalty area.
- You pretend an opponent has hit you in an attempt to get him a yellow or a red card.

When caught out for faking a move, you will force the referee to show you a yellow card for your improper behavior. Of course, this only applies if the referee or the linesman has actually picked up on the simulation.

The Referee Can Show You a Red Card in the Following Situations:

- You tackle an opponent who doesn't have the ball, or you physically hit/slap a player.
- You perform a hard tackle that injures the other player and the ref views it as a deliberate unnecessary attack.

- You deny the opposite team a direct chance of scoring using dirty tactics. This might be an unfair tackle or grabbing / pushing them away from the ball, or using your hand(s) to deflect a ball away from the goal line.

There is no Goal Counted from an Indirect Free Kick When:

You shoot the ball and it enters the opposite team's goal without touching any player from either side. In this case the goal won't count and the referee will award a free-kick against you.

A Penalty Is Not Counted in a Shootout When:

- The referee won't allow any of the two teams on the field to start taking penalties unless both sides have equal numbers of players. This means that if one team has fewer players than the other (maybe as a result of an injury or a player was sent off with a red card), then the other team must remove one (or more) players from their list of penalty shooters until the sides are equal in size.

- A ball does not count as "saved" by the goalkeeper until it stops moving completely.

The Rules for an Outside agent are:

I will first define what an "outside agent" is for those who might not be familiar with the term.

An outside agent, as defined by FIFA, is anyone not indicated on the team list as a player, substitute, or team official. Additionally, any player who has been sent off is also considered an outside agent.

- If an outside agent interferes with a play and there is a goal scored as a result of this play, then the referee will not count the goal if the outside agent was associated with the team that scored. However, if this agent is a member of, or is associated with, the team that had conceded the goal, or if the outside agent had entered the field but never interfered with the play, then the referee may officially consider the ball to be a goal.

The Ref Can Show Colored Cards When:

A referee has the authority to show any player a yellow card, or even send them off at any time during the game. He can do this from the moment of the first kick-off up until the game's closure.

This includes the half–time interval as well as any extra time played. His authority also extends to the penalty shootout and even if you`re sitting on the bench on the substitute list.

A Goal Will Be Disallowed When:

You`re in the "onside" position and you send a ball that enters the other teams goal. There`s a teammate of yours in the "offside" position when the goal was scored. In this situation, the referee will not count your goal in any of the two following situations:

- Your teammate (the one in the offside) touches the ball before it enters the goal.
- Your teammate interferes with the play by blocking an opponent (including the goalkeeper) from reaching the ball, or by standing in front of the goal and blocking the keeper from seeing it.

The last case happened in a game between Newcastle United and Manchester City. Here, Newcastle player, Cheick Tioté, scored a wonderful goal from outside the penalty area.

Unfortunately, the referee disallowed the goal because one of Tioté's teammates was blocking the keeper`s vision while standing in the offside position.

- A goal is not allowed when there's an unfair act of physical challenge, or obstruction, from you towards the opposition goalkeeper in the six yard area. Such actions may include something like stretching out to catch a cross or a high ball, for example. In this case, it would results in a foul for the opposite team.

- Any player showing unsporting behavior, like trying to verbally distract an opponent during a play, is punishable by the ref. Another example of unsporting behavior would be to change places with the goalkeeper during the game, and without the referee's permission.

Ending...

My final piece of advice to you is this: If you have dreams do not give up on them even if someone you look up to says you can't do a thing. Remember to always, always, always believe in yourself, even when stuff doesn't seem to be going according to plan, in fact, especially when things don't seem to be going according to plan. Remember too, there cannot be any progress without some failure and setbacks along the way, there just can't be. Be mindful of this whenever things get tough. If you don't believe in yourself then those who you need for encouragement and support won't be able to believe in you either. Be mindful of the fact that there is only one real failure in this life of ours, and that is the failure to try. I sincerely wish you all the very best in all your endeavors to succeed. Mirsad Hasic

About The Author

Mirsad writes all of his books in a unique style, constantly drawing connections between his past experiences and his reader's goals.

This unique approach means that you can avoid undergoing the same injuries, frustrations, and setbacks that he himself has endured over the years.

He can't produce the results for you, but what he can do is promise that you WILL reach your goals - guaranteed – providing you follow his tips and advice exactly as he outlines them in his books.

CPSIA information can be obtained at www.ICGtesting.com
Printed in the USA
LVOW10s2257201215

467329LV00022B/3128/P